Generous Genes

Raising Caring Kids in a Digital Age

Generous Genes *is a road map*
for parents, grandparents and
others for teaching kids—from
toddlers through teens—the
value of giving.

SUSAN CRITES PRICE
With JULIANNA M. PRICE

To Tom, my amazing partner in parenting, writing and life. SP

To Rick, for his love and patience, always. J

TABLE OF CONTENTS

INTRODUCTION

Nearly 15 years ago, I wrote *The Giving Family: Raising Our Children to Help Others* (Council on Foundations, 2000, rev. ed. 2003). A lot happened since then. For one thing, we've lived through the greatest economic downturn since the Depression. The ripple effect was felt by families everywhere—and provided many teachable moments for children—about wants vs. needs, living on less and pulling together to help others.

Another huge development has been the rise of social media. When I wrote *The Giving Family*, there was no Facebook, no Twitter, no YouTube. Today's array of digital tools provide children with new ways to connect with others interested in solving local or even global problems. Young people can use online tools to advocate for causes, raise and donate money and find volunteer jobs—including some that are completed online.

I grew up in a small town in Ohio. Like many Baby Boomers, I learned about the needs of my community mainly from my parents, my school and my church. My 29-year-old daughter Julie, a Millennial, is part of the generation called Digital Natives. She grew up using computers and the Internet. Today's children, Generation Z, can walk around with the Internet in their hands thanks to smart phones and tablets. No wonder people call today's young people the Always On generation. Parents are no longer the middlemen in helping their kids donate their time, talent and treasure (the three Ts)—there's an app for that. And now there's a fourth T—ties—because connections, especially online, can be a big asset for children trying to make a difference.

With so many options, children can be both inspired and confused about giving. This book will equip you to be a "generosity coach." For each stage of childhood, toddlers through teenagers, we'll give you strategies to talk to kids about giving, to help them identify their passions and guide—but not dictate—their choices of where and how to help. We cover how nonprofits, companies, schools and colleges can be allies with families in helping to raise the next generation to be givers. And we've included tips for teaching kids about money through allowances and other tools.

You'll find hundreds of ideas and resources, plus profiles of inspiring young people making a difference. We'll also share our personal stories, from the perspective of a Boomer mother and a Millennial daughter, about what works—and what doesn't—when you set out to raise a giving child. We hope our experiences will help inform your own.

CHAPTER 1

Parents As Generosity Coaches

Children are born with a conscience,
just not with the wisdom or experience to abide it.
That's where parenting comes in...

Bill Shore, author of *The Light of Conscience*

When our daughter Julie was born in 1985, my husband Tom and I were like most parents—we had dreams for her. We hoped she'd do well in school, make lasting friends, stay safe and healthy, find meaningful work and have a happy and fulfilling life. We believed that cultivating the values of caring and generosity was one key to having that life. It wasn't always easy.

We quickly discovered that young children have minds of their own, that they can be quite self-centered, and that there's never enough time to get through the "good parenting" to-do list. The outside world didn't make it easy either. The culture she was born into was one of rampant materialism. Advertisers were targeting kids as young as preschoolers because they saw these youngsters as a new demographic market. They assured little consumers that the best things in life were things: the latest toy, video game, breakfast cereal or outfit.

Julie also is an only child who grew up in an upper middle class neighborhood of Washington, DC with two doting parents. Her father and I didn't have a manual for how to avoid spoiling her. We just relied on our instincts and on the values that our own parents, products of The Great Depression and World War II, had instilled in us. We tried to teach her a value system that says part of being a responsible citizen—in a family, in a community, in the world—is caring about others. Some of the strategies we tried worked. Some didn't. But at least we had a foundation to build on, because Julie, like all children, was born with a genetic disposition to be generous. We just had to find ways to nurture that instinct.

From Julie

Growing up in Washington, DC, I saw tremendous wealth and horrific poverty all squished together into one city. As a very small child, I got to know my neighbors, and one of them was Bill.

Bill was a middle-aged homeless gentleman, who had struggled with schizophrenia his whole adult life. He was also a kind and funny fellow, and a part of our neighborhood. Bill lived for a time in one neighbor's basement, then in another neighbor's garage, and for longer stints on the street corner across from our house. His illness made it hard for him to stay in one place. I saw how our neighbors did their best to help Bill, including my mom and dad. Since Bill had no fixed address, he needed a place to have his Social Security disability checks delivered. My parents let him use our house as his mailing address. Whenever his check came, we put a flowerpot on the porch railing as a signal. He'd ring the doorbell, and usually stop to chat with us.

I'm sure it was a challenge for my parents to explain to a preschooler why anyone would have to live on the street. But they did it in a gentle, age-appropriate way. Many years later, as Bill grew older, he realized he could no longer live on the streets in the harsh winter weather. His illness made it hard for him to trust the organizations that could help him, but he finally began working with a caseworker at our neighborhood resource center for the homeless. They nominated him for special housing, and my dad wrote a recommendation letter for him. After all those years on the street, Bill finally got an apartment—and his own mailing address.

Nature vs. Nurture

Science has determined that humans are not born selfish. Numerous researchers conducting behavioral studies on babies and toddlers are finding that they are born with tendencies to care about and want to help others. That may be hard to believe when you find yourself coping with a demanding two-year-old—or 13-year-old. But researchers at Yale University, for example, have done numerous experiments with 18-month-olds, including one in which the experimenter drops something and makes it appear that the item is out of reach. Nearly all the toddlers, without being asked, will retrieve it and give it back, surprising even to the researchers who predicted the toddlers would keep the item.[1]

Darwin's theory of the survival of the fittest never explained why people would risk their lives to save someone else. Later scientists theorized that altruism is a way individuals improve their own prospects "by contributing to the well-being of a strong collective."[2]

Now, scientists able to measure changes in brain activity in adults have identified circuits that control nurturing impulses. They've also found that giving to charity triggers chemicals in the brain that create pleasurable feelings. Bottom line: You've got the raw material in your child's genetic instinct to be generous. Teach them to give, and they'll become compassionate as well as happy individuals, reasons enough to incorporate giving into your family's daily life.

The Power of Parents

"Can you hear me now?" That line from a phone company ad might characterize your relationship with your children. Are they listening? Do they get what you are trying to convey about how they can be givers—and why they should? Researchers have tackled that question, too. And they confirm that parents are the biggest influence

---

[1] *"Are Babies Born Good?" by Abigail Tucker,* Smithsonian Magazine, *January, 2013.*
[2] Wall Street Journal, *"Hard Wired for Giving," by Elizabeth Svoboda, Aug. 31, 2013*

on whether children donate time or money. For example, Indiana University's Women's Philanthropy Institute—in partnership with the UN Foundation—released a study in 2013 of kids between ages 8 and 19. The researchers found that parents play an important role in raising children who become charitable adults. Among the key findings: talking to children about charity has a greater impact on children's giving than role modeling alone, and that such conversations are equally effective regardless of a parent's income level or the child's gender, race or age. Even when youngsters become teenagers, parents still have influence—though some teens might not admit it. A study by Do Something (a popular online volunteering venue primarily for tweens and teens) found that, while the influence of friends on children's volunteering increases as they age, family is still slightly more influential than their friends are, even among middle and high school students. That's more evidence that early nurturing of your children's giving instincts can have lasting impact.

Anyone Can be a Philanthropist

People often think the term "philanthropist" refers to someone old and rich. Not so. The term literally means love of mankind, and any altruistic acts can fall within that definition. People with little or no money can still help others through acts of caring and kindness. And when a lot of people pool their acts of giving, that can have a big impact on a problem. We use the terms "charity" as well as "philanthropy" in this book. Some people make a distinction between the two—that charity is designed to meet an immediate need, providing meals for homeless people for example, and that philanthropy tries to solve root problems so people aren't homeless. But the common understanding of these words is similar enough that we use both to mean giving. The sentiments haven't changed, but the methods of giving have expanded markedly—thanks to the Internet.

Time, Talent, Treasure...and Ties

The tools kids can use to practice digital philanthropy, especially social media, were unheard of when Julie was young. The Internet has in some ways removed parents as the middlemen for their children's philanthropy. Young people can learn about causes, share their favorites with others, raise money, find volunteer opportunities, play games that teach social good and advocate for change through online petitions. They can text a donation on their mobile phone or ask all the friends in their social network to sponsor them in a walk to aid the homeless. To the trifecta of giving—time, talent and treasure—we've now added ties, because of all the connections children and adults have through social media.

The Internet has brought the world to our doors. Today's kids learn about the needs of a village in Africa as easily as a neighborhood in their hometown. As users keep getting younger (who hasn't seen a pre-schooler playing games on Mom's or Dad's cell phone?), parents will need to keep up with their children's online world. In particular, we can help them identify scams and teach them to give with both their hearts and their heads by checking out organizations' effectiveness in using charitable dollars.

TIP: *Chapter 4 will help you monitor, guide and encourage your children's online philanthropic activity, while also directing them to real-world—not just virtual—giving experiences.*

What's In It for Us?

This may seem like an odd question. In theory, most parents would say that teaching kids to be generous is part of their roles. No one sets out to raise a selfish child. Yet, when it comes to fitting altruism into our daily routines, life gets in the way. There are jobs and school and sports and music lessons and a million other claims on a family's time. I understand that; I've been there. But encouraging generosity can be worked into everyday life in lots of small ways that don't take much time and can have a big payoff. Wait: Payoff, you ask? Shouldn't we be doing charity out of the goodness of our hearts?

True altruism is giving without expecting anything in return. But let's face it: we are more motivated to do things when there is a reward. If you volunteer as a family—or your older kids volunteer with friends or on their own—the people they help are benefiting. But here are just a few of the many benefits your family receives:

- Families spend quality time together.

- Children learn empathy and caring.

- Volunteer jobs can provide creative outlets.

- Volunteers learn problem solving.

- Volunteers feel useful, especially when they are giving back for help they've received.

- Research shows that volunteering improves people's physical and mental health.

- Children who volunteer are less likely to engage in risky behavior.

- It's a chance for kids to learn new skills and gain confidence. Teens might even learn a skill they could use in a job someday.

- Volunteering fosters friendships and understanding by bringing different people together. For example: high school geeks with football players, elementary school students with senior citizens, children from different cultures or economic backgrounds.

- Volunteers forget their own troubles when they focus on helping others who may be facing even greater hardships (the perfect antidote for teen angst!).

- High schoolers can beef up their college applications; a volunteer job might even lead them to a career path.

- Volunteers have fun. That's why they call it the joy of giving!

What About Giving Money?

Most of the benefits of volunteering listed above can also apply to donating money. When we talk about giving in this book, we are including the sharing of money, time and special skills. But since most young children don't have cash to donate to charity—and some families don't either—giving time may be your primary focus, especially when your kids are young. It doesn't need to be. In Chapter 3, we go into this in more detail, but it's worth making a couple of points here.

First, children don't have to have their own money to donate; they can raise funds for their favorite causes. They still can do it the old-fashioned way—with odd jobs or lemonade stands, for example—but many 21st century kids are also quite savvy about raising money through their social media networks.

Second, even a tiny amount can help, especially when pooled with other donations. One classic example is the annual Penny Harvest in New York City, during which school children across the city collect thousands of dollars in pennies. Their classrooms then become mini-foundations, with the kids learning about various nonprofits and deciding where to give their portion of the "harvest." The program also engages the children, ages 4 through 14, in neighborhood service projects so they learn about volunteering, too. The Penny Harvest has now spread to a few other cities.

TIP: *Go to the website of Common Cents, the organization that runs the Penny Harvest (commoncents.org), to read the inspiring story of its founding, when a four-year-old asked her dad if they could take a homeless man home.*

No One Size Fits All

Even if generosity is instinctive, all kids are different in how they embody it. Some like to volunteer but not part with their money. Some are too shy to volunteer but happy to raise money online. Siblings often vary widely in how generous they are. Even an individual child's interest in giving

PROFILE IN GENEROSITY:

Bursting the Bubble

Lana Volftsun provides a good example of how a strong spirit of giving can take hold at any age. Growing up sheltered in suburban Northern Virginia, she had an epiphany at age 12. "I had my bat mitzvah [a coming-of-age ceremony for Jewish girls], and my mom told me I had to give away all the money I had gotten as gifts. I was really mad." Her mom decided to start a giving circle for other kids having their bat or bar mitzvahs [for boys] so they could pool their money and make donations together. "That experience changed my whole trajectory," Volftsun recalled. She describes her life to that point as "living in a bubble." When the giving circle kids visited various nonprofits they were considering for grants, "my bubble burst. We learned about people with no food, with health problems, about abused kids, and people who didn't have clean drinking water. I realized I could make a difference in the world."

It's also worth noting that Volftsun's mother's project to help kids put their bar and bat mitzvah money to good use turned into an ongoing and much larger effort through Jewish congregations across the Washington region. And, when Volftsun grew up, she became executive director of the Giving Circles Fund, a network of online giving circles.

can fluctuate at different ages. Like a good sports coach, a generosity coach recognizes each child's differences and works with that. This book contains lots of approaches you can try to see what works, while you continue to make clear that giving is a value in your family, and that everyone is expected to do their part in some way.

Your coaching role will change too over time. With young children—toddlers through early elementary school—you'll typically volunteer together. When they are tweens and teens, they usually want to volunteer with their friends—although they might still enjoy an occasional family volunteer outing, especially if it's a long-standing tradition such as helping prepare a Thanksgiving meal at a soup kitchen. But no matter what the age or stage of your child, you have a role to play in encouraging, providing inspiration and just keeping the conversation going.

Seven Keys to Generosity Coaching

- **Start young.** The earlier you start, the easier giving will become a habit. How early? Start the first time your child says the word "Mine."

  Note: This doesn't mean that, if your child is a teenager, it's too late to start nurturing generous genes. It may be harder to get their attention, but it's still worth the effort.

- **Be a role model.** Do your kids know about the volunteering you did as child or do now? Do you tell them about the organizations you give money to and how you decide among the many who ask you to donate? How you handle giving can help them make their own philanthropic decisions.

- Help them **find their passions** but let them decide. Kids might do a volunteer project you enlist them for once in a while. But they will be much more engaged if it's something they feel passionate about. (See Chapter 5 for more on identifying passions.)

- **Support their use of the Internet** as a tool for philanthropy, but not as a substitute for giving of themselves up close and personal.

- **Cultivate an attitude of gratitude.** We aren't always the givers; often we are the beneficiaries of someone else's kindness. Teach your children to show their thanks. At the dinner table or before bed, ask them to name something they are thankful for that day. Consider other acts, too, such as baking cookies and delivering them to your local fire fighters, to show you appreciate what they do for your community.

- **Don't underestimate your children.** This book is full of stories of ordinary kids who have done extraordinary things with their philanthropy. Even very young children are capable of helping— and should be expected to do so.

- **Look for teachable moments.** Read books or see movies together that have a giving theme and discuss them afterward. Devote dinner conversations or long cars rides to questions like "What kind thing did you do today?" or "If you had $1,000 to give to charity, what would you give it to?" And when you go to a children's museum, zoo or other favorite place run by a nonprofit, explain that it's there for all to enjoy because people donate time and money to support it.

Digital Deed: To jump-start the conversation, try the Central Carolina Community Foundation's Talk About Giving game. This set of 60 glossy cards contains simple yet thought-provoking questions in four categories: Money Matters, Family Matters, Giving Matters and What Matters to Me? The game can be ordered at talkaboutgiving.org.

Saying Thanks

I recently read a comment by a 20-something that her generation doesn't do handwritten thank-you notes. That may be true in general, but Julie writes thank-you notes because I instilled in her from a young age that such notes are common courtesy for acts of kindness. This is especially true for gifts that arrive in the mail, because everyone likes to get handwritten mail (a rarity these days), and gift-givers want to know that the present actually arrived and was appreciated. (Don't tell Miss Manners, but I sometimes email thank-you notes, depending on the gift-giver and the situation, but writing real notes is still a good practice to teach children when they are young—and to maintain as an adult.)

TIP:

Let your children pick out some cute thank-you notes. If they are too young to write, they can decorate notes with stickers or drawings. You might also enclose the child's photo. Once your children are old enough to write, give them some sample language. For times when there will be multiple gifts—holidays or birthdays, for example—help your child create a chart to keep track of who gave them what, and check off when the note is written and sent.

Sidelines Coaches—Grandparents and Extended Family

Parents aren't the only family members who can help to raise giving children. Grandparents can encourage their grandchildren by sharing stories of who helped them when they were growing up, how they help others and causes they love. They also can provide support, such as offering to match donations their grandchildren make from their allowances. When grandparents, aunts, uncles or other relatives live nearby, you can invite them to join your family's volunteering projects. Grandparents also might enjoy volunteering with their grandchildren alone, creating a special bond over a shared experience.

Digital Deed: **Family history is a tie that binds. Kids can interview grandparents or other relatives and put together a recording as a lasting gift for the family. The Story Corps website (storycorps.org) has sample questions. You can even make a recording that will be added to the Story Corps archive.**

Allies to Parents

Older kids will find mentors beyond the family. Teachers, scout leaders, sports coaches and others who have contact with your children can add to the lessons you are imparting at home. Some schools require community service. Colleges are even getting into the act, sponsoring service projects and offering courses in grantmaking.

If your family participates in a religious congregation, that's another place your child will be exposed to giving. Many of us Baby Boomers were raised in religious institutions but stopped going once we became adults. When we became parents, some of us returned to houses of worship. We wanted our children to learn a faith tradition and also have one more place where their generosity genes could be nurtured. All major religions have some tenet that addresses the obligation to help the poor and to be kind to others. Many also emphasize being good stewards of the earth.

We Shouldn't Shelter Our Kids

Washington is a city of wide income gaps, and such gaps exist within other cities, too. Kids in one part of town often have no idea how different life is in other neighborhoods.

An enthusiastic girl I judged to be about 12 came to our door one day and asked an odd question: Did we have any used denim jeans to donate? She explained that she and her classmates at our nearby middle school were collecting them to give to teens living in homeless shelters. I was surprised to see she had already gathered a huge bag full. The next day I read in our newspaper that her school was teaching students about homelessness by bringing in speakers who have lived on the streets. Seeing the real faces of homelessness, poverty, mental illness and other challenges was a revelation to those mostly well-off children. With understanding came a desire to take action. Collecting jeans was just one of the projects the classmates took on.

Parents are sometimes reluctant to expose their children to soup kitchens, nursing homes with dementia patients, facilities for kids with disabilities or other challenging situations for fear their children will be upset. Sometimes I think it's we adults who have the hang-up. While we may feel sad, guilty or powerless in the face of such complex issues, kids are less likely to overthink a situation and focus instead on the simple act of helping someone else.

The Internet puts the world's problems at their fingertips, and that can overwhelm children. The phrase "change the world," seems daunting. Tell them that they can start by making a small difference in another person's life right in their own community, then work up from there. Mother Teresa said: "If you can't feed a hundred people, then feed just one."

Real life, not just virtual experiences, is an important way for children to discover that all of us are part of the human race, and it is only circumstances—such as being born into the "lucky gene pool"— that make some people's lives comfortable and others' lives filled with hardship.

TIP: *DoSomething.org is an excellent online community that engages young people in various projects. For example, they have an annual campaign asking teens to bring gently used jeans to an Aeropostale store in their local mall. The company distributes the donations to family shelters, where jeans are the Number One thing teens ask for. Do Something's project ideas are available on the Internet, but the actions are hands-on.*

A Giving Pledge for the Rest of Us

In 2010, Warren Buffett and Bill and Melinda Gates got a bunch of billionaires to sign a Giving Pledge, promising to donate at least half of their wealth to philanthropy. By 2014, more than 125 individuals and couples had signed the pledge. But philanthropy has never been restricted to the rich. In fact, people in the lowest income categories donate a higher percent of their income than people in the wealthiest.

One way to make sure your family is serious about giving is through a measurable commitment. Why not make your own Giving Pledge? If your kids are young, they can be part of a Family Giving Pledge. Older ones can make their own. It can be as simple as "We pledge as a family to volunteer together five hours a month." In this book, you'll find hundreds of ideas you can jot on your calendar for incorporating giving into your daily life, including holiday celebrations, birthdays, even vacations.

Keeping Track

If your family is going to set a goal, you can also try some easy ways to keep track other than allocating hours on your calendar. When kids are younger, you can make a family giving scrapbook. Have your children draw pictures or take photos of your volunteer activities and make a page for each one that includes "how we helped" and "what we learned." (Note that photos involving help for disadvantaged people can raise privacy concerns, so don't take pictures without permission.) An alternative to photos is to clip pictures from magazines or newspapers. For example work in a soup kitchen can be represented by a photo of canned goods. The idea isn't to make a beautiful book—it's to engage your kids in recording their giving and talking about it while you do.

Older kids can keep a giving journal noting donations of time or money to which organizations or causes. A periodic review can help your sons or daughters figure out the impact of their giving and whether they are focusing their efforts on things they are really passionate about.

PROFILE IN GENEROSITY:

What Bracelet Are You Wearing?

Many of us who came of age during the Vietnam War wore metal bracelets bearing the name of a soldier who was missing in action or a prisoner of war. Usually, we didn't know the people whose names we wore; we just wanted to share the hope that someday they would come home. Some did. Julie's generation started sporting Lance Armstrong's Live Strong yellow wrist bands to raise money for cancer research. Millions were sold at $1 each. That success spawned a rainbow of wrist bands for all kinds of causes. Here's a variation on the wrist band that leads to daily action:

San Diego-area mom Sara Schairer is raising her 7-year-old daughter to be compassionate. "She's gone with me to feed the home-less, for example, and giving has been a part of her life," Schairer explained. But she also knows that "it's sometimes difficult for busy families to incorporate giving in their daily lives. You have to make a conscious effort."

Thus was born the "Compassion It" bracelet, which has created a global movement of people engaged in compassionate acts. It's two-sided and reversible so you can start the day with one side out and then when you do something compassionate, flip to the other side. "Compassion becomes a verb," she said.

Her first batch of 1,000 bracelets was used to raise money for three families in a small town in Illinois who lost three teens—two to suicide and one to a car crash—in three weeks. Another town in Missouri used the bracelets to unite around compassionate acts after the suicide of a 13-year-old girl who had been bullied. More than 40,000 bracelets have created compassionate actions in 43 countries.

One high schooler who has the bracelet wrote Schairer that it "has completely changed my life. I now find myself reaching out to strangers and friends every day with compassionate words and gestures. Turning it over is the highlight of my day." Some bracelet-wearing families share their acts of compassion each night at dinner.

Schairer's nonprofit organization sells the bracelets in pairs so that your first compassionate act is to give one bracelet away. School groups and others can buy the bracelets at substantial quantity discounts to sell as fundraisers while also creating a ripple of generous acts. Proceeds from wristband sales go toward the organization's compassion education programs. (compassionit.com)

TIP: *Mission statements are essential for organizations, but they can be useful for families and individuals, too. A family mission statement can be a paragraph or two about your beliefs, values and what you hope to accomplish. Similarly, your older children can write personal mission statements. Ask them who their heroes are, what they love to do, what causes they care about, what talents and skills they have to offer and how they'd like to apply them to help their community or the world.*

Praise Kids for their Good Acts

You've heard that virtue is its own reward. But we also know that it's nice to be recognized for doing something good. Children, especially, feel that way. Praising your kids for their good deeds reinforces the behavior— so they'll be more likely to repeat it—and it lets them know this is something you value. Researchers Joan E. Grusec and Erica Redler found that it's more effective to praise the behavior behind the act of giving rather than the act itself. Tell a child her actions show she's a helpful person, and she'll internalize helpfulness as part of her identity.

TIP: *There are a number of recognition programs for outstanding volunteers and fund raisers. The President's Council on Service and Civil Participation sends Volunteer Service Award certificates and pins to people as young as 5 who volunteer specified numbers of hours. The Prudential Spirit of Community Award, in partnership with the National Association of Secondary School Principals, honors middle and high school students for outstanding service. Kohl's stores have a nationwide competition—Kohl's Kids Care—that rewards school-age volunteers across the country with scholarships and prizes. Local chapters of the Association of Fund Raising Professionals sometimes honor outstanding youth in their annual award programs.*

How Generosity Helps Kids Cope With Scary Situations

Beloved children's television host Mr. Rogers once said: "When I was a boy and would see scary things on the news, my mother would say to me 'Look for the helpers. You will always find people who are helping.'"

I saw this quote on Facebook the day of the Boston Marathon bombing. There were plenty of images of helpers in the news coverage: runners and race volunteers as well as first responders aiding the injured without regard to whether there could be more bombs. Some runners kept on running—to hospitals to donate blood.

Kids will inevitably be exposed to scary stories through the media and the Internet. One reason these situations are scary even from afar is that bombings, earthquakes and floods, for example, seem beyond our control. We may not be able to stop them, but there is always a way to help, to focus on what is in our control.

TIP: *If you want to make a donation to aid disaster victims, involve your children in a conversation about which organization you'll send the contribution to.*

PROFILE IN GENEROSITY:

Coping by Sharing a Talent

The weekend following Sept. 11, 2001, I was walking through Georgetown when I spotted a young girl, whom I guessed to be about 10, standing on a street corner and playing "God Bless America" on her clarinet. At her feet was a sign that said "Patriotic Songs for the Red Cross" and next to it was a bucket holding a big pile of $5s, $10s and $20s. A man I assumed was her dad stood off to the side looking on with an expression of pride. Many of the rest of us in her impromptu audience were teary. Her use of her talent to help the victims was just what Washington needed that day—a sense of hope in our next generation. Read any advice columnist and you find frequent references to the antidote for coping with emotionally tough times: Forget your troubles by finding ways to give to others.

TIP: *For help with discussing frightening events with your children, see parenting expert Anne Pleshette Murphy's guide written at the time of the Haiti earthquake (http://tinyurl.com/m38g44h).*

PROFILE IN GENEROSITY:

The Power of Half

*I met Kevin Selwen at a philanthropy conference in 2009. He was there
to share a remarkable story of one family's act of giving. The following
year, he and his teenage daughter Hannah co-authored a book,* The
Power of Half: One Family's Decision to Stop Taking and Start Giving
Back *(Houghton Mifflin Harcourt, 2010), which received much positive
media coverage. It is a book I have recommended countless times, not
only because it's inspiring, but also because it takes you inside this family as they struggle with the challenges of acting on their values, making
sacrifices, deciding where their money would have the most impact and
dealing with the sometimes negative reactions of friends and strangers.*

*Their story started in Atlanta in 2006 when Hannah, then
14, and her dad were in their car stopped at a traffic light. Through
her passenger window Hannah saw a man holding a sign that said
HUNGRY, HOMELESS, PLEASE HELP. Glancing the other way, she
saw a Mercedes convertible. Pointing to the Mercedes, Hannah said,
"Dad, if that man had a less nice car, that man there could have a
meal." Writing in her journal later, Hannah said that moment changed
her life. It also profoundly changed her family's.*

*Kevin and Hannah joined her mother Joan and younger brother
Joseph at the dinner table that night and related the incident. That
conversation led to many more about why people are hungry, what
the Selwens could do to change things, and also about the meaning of
money. It wasn't a new subject. The family had engaged in plenty of
volunteering. Hunger issues were Hannah's passion. Beginning in fifth*

grade she regularly prepared and served meals to homeless people. This time, she wanted to do more to address the world's inequities. As she continued to press her case, her mother finally responded: "What do you want to do, sell our house?" She was serious.

The Selwens were a well-off family living in a 6,500 square foot historic home in Atlanta, with both kids attending private schools. Together they decided to take the bold—some said crazy—step of selling their dream house and moving to one half the size so they could give away half the sales price. Eventually, they were able to donate $800,000 to help villages in Ghana become self-sustaining.

No question it's an inspiring story. But, as with most things, it's complicated. The Selwen family's willingness to candidly share their own struggles is what makes this book so useful. First was their decision-making process. Joseph was not on board at first. He liked his large bedroom in the only home he'd really known. When he was finally convinced, the Selwens faced many more decisions around giving away the money. Kevin and Joan decided to flip the parent authority model and let the kids have a sense of ownership in the project by giving them an equal vote in the decisions. The regular family meetings were long and lively. Finding time for them was tricky.

There were unexpected challenges. Reactions to their project from some of their friends and even close relatives were mixed and occasionally quite negative, leading to uncomfortable distances in those relationships. Others were so supportive that even their real estate agent donated to the cause. Although the Selwens found and bought a smaller house quickly, it took more than two years to sell the big house in a down economy. Paring down their furniture and other belongings was a project in itself. Meanwhile, Kevin's business failed. Still they persevered with what came to be known as their adventure.

After moving, the Selwens discovered an advantage in the smaller house: Tighter quarters promoted more interaction. The family spent more time together around the piano when it was moved from a back room in the big house to the living room in their new home. The ping pong table occupied a more prominent place—and inspired more family play time—in the smaller house. The family meetings added to their shared experiences. Kevin wrote that while they were helping the world a little bit, they transformed their relationships with each other. "And that has been a real surprise."

To me the most fascinating sections of the book describe the conversations about what to do with the money, because they quickly learned that giving effectively isn't easy. Where would a gift have the most impact? Which nonprofit would do the best job with it? How involved did they want to be? The eventual choice: the Hunger Project, specifically the organization's work in Ghana, a country the Selwens had to look up on a map. The teenagers' thought-processes took the adults in interesting directions. Any serious philanthropist will find lessons here. The story concludes with the family's trip to Ghana to see their money at work. We all can learn from the descriptions of their family's first experience in the developing world, and how it felt—especially to teenagers—to be out of their comfort zone, meeting people they were helping.

The Power of Half is not just a book for parents. Adolescents enjoy it too. Kevin and Hannah are deft storytellers. But be forewarned. In a New York Times *book review, Columnist Nicholas Kristof wrote:* "It's a book that frankly, I'd be nervous about leaving around where my own teenage kids might find it. An impressionable child reads this and the next thing you know, your whole family is out on the street."

TIP: *The Selwens don't expect others to do what they did. But they chose giving "half" because it was a measurable goal and more meaningful than just committing to give "more." In sidebars called "Hannah's Take," scattered throughout the book, Hannah helps kids figure out ways they can commit to give half by identifying their time, talent and treasure. For example, they can halve the time they spend playing video games and volunteer instead. One of her friends committed to donating half her babysitting money. It's a compelling idea. The same year the book came out, Warren Buffett and Bill Gates started signing up billionaires to the Giving Pledge, asking them to give at least half of their wealth to charity.*

CHAPTER 2:

Buddy, Can You Spare Some Time?

I always wondered why somebody doesn't do
something about that. Then I realized
I was somebody...

Actress Lily Tomlin

Now that we've given you the "why" of sharing time, talent and treasure, let's focus more on the "how." In this chapter, we'll cover the time and talent part. In Chapter 3, we'll discuss giving money.

The great thing about volunteering is that anybody can do it. You don't have to have money. You just have to be motivated—both to make the time and then to find ways to use that time for the good of others. Keep in mind that kids, like adults, are more motivated to volunteer if they enjoy it.

A friend of mine was lamenting to me one day that her high school daughter wasn't doing any volunteering. I knew that her daughter, who had a lovely singing voice, performed sometimes at nursing homes, and I pointed that out. The mother dismissed this, saying "Oh, but she enjoys that." Apparently, my friend thought singing didn't count because real volunteering involves sacrifice. It can, and to some degree, it does. But it should also be rewarding in some way—giving kids that glow inside when they have accomplished something by helping someone else. The more they enjoy it, the more they'll want to do it.

Is It Really Volunteering If You Make Them Do It?

Should you force your child to volunteer? While I don't think nagging
or preaching work when you are trying to encourage altruism, you can
communicate that your family expects everyone to share their time,
talent and treasure. If you start them young by volunteering as a family,
it's more likely to become a habit. I've also heard countless stories from
parents whose kids grumbled about going on a volunteer project with
their parents and siblings, only to end up enjoying it. And they might
as well get used to it, because many teens will go to schools that require
community service for graduation.

Pre-teens and teenagers will want to volunteer with peers. Your
role changes to coach and cheerleader. You can give them ideas, help
them identify things they really care about, encourage them, praise them
and drive them to volunteer jobs. But don't be tempted to pick projects
for them. (I've tried it and, trust me, it doesn't work.) Your passions aren't
necessarily theirs. Some adolescents like working with young children;
others prefer senior citizens. Some are fine with indoor projects, while
others would rather be outside. Some may want to volunteer for one-time
events, and others will like an ongoing commitment. Some may want to
do something their friends are enthusiastic about, regardless of whether
they are themselves. And that's okay, too, because any exposure to
volunteering is worthwhile.

TIP: *Chapter 5 helps you help your children identify their passions
and offers dozens of ideas for projects your kids can do, either
through an organization or on their own.*

Choosing a Volunteer Project—Questionnaire*

Use this questionnaire to help your older children find volunteer projects that fit them.

- Why do you want to volunteer?
- List your hobbies, interests and skills. Would you like to use any of them in a volunteer job?
- What did you like or dislike about past volunteer experiences?
- Are there new skills you would like to learn from volunteering?
- How much time can you offer?
- Do you prefer a short-term or long-term project?
- When do you want to volunteer? (After school, on weekends, etc.)
- Do you enjoy working one-on-one with people (mentoring or tutoring, for instance)?
- Do you prefer working with friends or classmates or on your own?
- Do you like working outside or inside?

Next, research some possible volunteer opportunities, then ask:

- Is the mission of the organization something you really care about?
- How much time commitment do they require?
- Does the schedule fit with yours?
- Will the projects fulfill your motivations for volunteering?

Adapted from The Giving Family: Raising Our Children to Help Others *by Susan Crites Price (Council on Foundations, 2000)*

What's Your Talent?

Focusing on something your child is really good at is a great way to help him or her find fulfilling volunteer work. When they were in middle school, for example, one of Julie's friends—a computer whiz—volunteered at our senior citizens center, teaching seniors to use computers. Older kids with sports skills can help coach beginning players. Book lovers can shelve books at the library. Artistic children can help paint murals. Kids who love to bake can make cookies for someone who needs a little boost. Children who are good at chess can teach younger ones in their after-school program. As your children's generosity coach, you can help them identify their talents, then help them find ways to put the talents to good use.

PROFILE IN GENEROSITY:

Let's Put on a Show!

Growing up, I watched countless old Judy Garland/Mickey Rooney movies in which the stars, faced with some kind of financial crisis, decide to put on a show to raise money. It was a great excuse to work song and dance numbers into the films, and it never got old. That's what the Teen Angel Project (TeenAngelProject.org) in the Washington, DC, area reminds me of—except these kids get paid in smiles. Started in 2012, the troupe of middle and high school singers and dancers performs for free at nursing homes, shelters, military rehab facilities, hospitals, retirement communities or wherever there are people in need of cheer. An affiliated group of elementary schoolers is called TAP, Jr. This concept could be replicated in any town with a few dedicated young people who love to perform.

Don't Assume Your Way Is the Right Way

It's so easy for us parents to assume we need to teach kids how everything should be done. Often, we could learn more from them. Case in point: A friend of mine talked her middle schooler into going to a soup kitchen with her to serve a meal. He wasn't very enthusiastic, but she prevailed. Once there, she could see he was enjoying it—maybe a little too much. "He wasn't being efficient," my Type A friend recalled. Her son wasn't working as fast as other servers because he was chatting with the clients as he dished out portions on their plates. If he thought someone looked extra hungry, he'd give them extra helpings, something the soup kitchen managers don't endorse because of the need to stretch the food.

When my friend and her son left the kitchen that night, some of the diners were still hanging around outside. They greeted her son by name. He smiled and returned their greetings with a "Hi, Joe," or "So long, Mary." My friend was amazed and a little embarrassed. "In that short time, he'd gotten to know these people as human beings," she said, "while I was just doing the job with my usual efficiency."

Finding Places to Volunteer

Finding volunteer opportunities with nonprofits can be tricky for families with young children. Minneapolis-based author Jenny Friedman, who wrote *The Busy Family's Guide to Volunteering* (Robins Lane Press 2003), founded the nonprofit organization Doing Good Together (doinggoodtogether.org) to help families practice kindness with children from the very young through adolescence.

"There aren't as many opportunities out there for families to volunteer," Friedman said. "They call organizations and say 'we want to bring our three-year-old' and the organization says 'we don't take three-year-olds.'" Additionally, it's hard for families with young children to make time for volunteering. "Families are overstressed," Friedman said. "The last thing they want to hear is that they ought to be doing one more thing."

That's why she added the Big-Hearted Families program. "We make it really simple to start doing projects with your kids—even 15 minutes at your kitchen table, just to get the conversation started. Parents are always looking for fun things to do with their kids. We don't want it to be only about fun but, if it isn't, kids won't do it."

At the website, families find a collection of tools, including project ideas and printable resources. "We believe that every family can give back, with children of any age, in whatever time you have to give," Friedman said.

 **Sign up for the Doing Good Together monthly e-newsletter at doinggoodtogether.org, and you'll receive a host of creative ideas for families who want to help others. "Like" them on Facebook, and you'll get ideas even more often. The website has additional resources.**

Families sometimes have difficulty identifying projects that appeal to their children's different ages and interests. And pre-teens and teens may not be all that keen on hanging out with their parents. Still, participating in something together can be rewarding. If you spend your weekends at your children's sports events, for example, your family might really love volunteering together at a Special Olympics event. Or find a time when you are together for another reason, such as a family vacation, and brainstorm some ways to incorporate giving. (See Volunteer Vacations later in this chapter.) Let the kids take a leading role in generating ideas—and let siblings take turns picking.

Online Volunteer Matchmaking

Several Internet sites help match volunteers with jobs available at nonprofits. The challenge is to find jobs that aren't limited to adults.

- **Volunteer Match** (volunteermatch.org) lets you sort by distance from where you live and by causes such as animals, literacy, environment and homeless/hunger. From the "I care about…" box, click "advanced search" to reveal filters that let you sort by projects suitable for "kids" and for "teens."

- **All For Good** (allforgood.org) is another volunteer hub, this one operated by Points of Light. If you see an opportunity that interests your family, read the posting to learn if kids are allowed, or contact the organizer by email.

- **HandsOn Network** (handsonnetwork.org), also part of Points of Light, represents approximately 250 volunteer action centers in cities across the country. Click on the interactive map to see if there is one in your area.

- **Volunteen Nation** (volunteennation.org), run by young people for young people—middle, high school and college students—can connect your kids to volunteer opportunities and sources of grants and scholarships.

TIP: *If your family or your teens have specific interests or skills to offer and don't see the ideal position posted, approach a nonprofit with your idea. But let the organization determine what would be most helpful. What you think it needs may not be what they can use, for a variety of reasons that may have nothing to do with the merit of your idea.*

Before You Go

Before signing on to volunteer with an organization, either as a family or individual, make sure you check what ages the organization will take, what training is provided, how they handle safety issues, what requirements they have—such as dress and hours during which the service is needed—and who will be supervising the volunteers. Ask, too, about the amount of time they expect from volunteers. Some require certain time commitments because of the investment they make in volunteer training.

Another key part of successful volunteering is preparing your kids before they go. Talk about who they are going to help, what tasks they are going to perform, how long it will take and so forth. If your family is going to deliver toys to a homeless shelter, explain to your children that the kids in the shelter are no different from them except for circumstances beyond their control. If it's a food pantry, you can talk with your children about the many reasons people sometimes need help with food, such as job loss or illness—not because they are lazy.

TIP: *The American Girl doll Kit Kittredge was the subject of a feature film set in the Great Depression. Kit learns how hard times can hit anybody and why we shouldn't make assumptions about people who need help. It has a compelling plot—even interesting for adults—and strong male characters, too.* **Kit Kittredge: An American Girl** *is available through Netflix and other services.*

Time for reflection afterward is also important. Here are some sample questions to discuss:

- What did you like best? Least?
- What did you learn that surprised you?
- Did anything make you uncomfortable? Why?
- Is there some way we could have done the work better?
- Would you like to repeat this project, or would you rather try something new?

PROFILE IN GENEROSITY:

A Project a Week

The Brown family of Fort Wayne, Indiana—dad Aaron, mom Erica, and daughters Kelsi and Makenna—decided in 2011 to do a different volunteer project every week. They called it Impact 52, and as of this writing, they are still going strong. The Browns also blog about their volunteer adventures (impact52.org), so you can follow their work and get ideas for researching and choosing your own charities or causes. Their slogan is "Inspiring Change One Week at a Time."

What Teens Want from Volunteering

For many teens, friends are the doorway to volunteering. Aria Finger, Chief Operating Officer of Do Something, said it doesn't matter that teens volunteer for something just because their friends are. "If they have a good time, they'll still have positive associations with volunteering." As they become exposed to organizations through volunteering, Finger said, they'll become more discerning. "Teens can ask themselves: Am I making an impact? Is the organization well run? Am I excited to tell people about it? Was I given enough information?"

Do Something's 2012 poll of more than 4,300 young people nationwide (the first national survey of its kind) explored what causes them to take action. Having friends that volunteer regularly is the primary factor influencing a teen's volunteering habits. Among the key findings:

- More than 70 percent of young people with friends who regularly volunteer also volunteer.

- Young people want to volunteer with people their age.

- Lack of time is the number one reason teens give for not volunteering.

- Young people want volunteer opportunities that are close to home, but not at home.

- Short activities that allow for different levels of engagement are best.

PROFILE IN GENEROSITY:

Just Do Something

With 3.1 million members, Do Something (dosomething.org) is one of the largest online organizations for young people interested in social change. Do Something spearheads national campaigns with three rules: none of the projects requires money, an adult or a car. Chief Operating Officer Aria Finger said most Do Something members are high school or college age, but some middle schoolers participate, too.

Young people love the site because it speaks to them. Founder Nancy Lublin is listed as CEO and Chief Old Person. Everything about the site is youth-focused, irreverent and fun, but the organization is having significant impact.

What can parents do? Encourage your teens to join Do Something and take action on a cause that fits their interests. With 11 cause areas—such as animals, homelessness, education, bullying, the environment—Do Something is bound to offer an activity that appeals to your children. Participants can post information about their own successful projects. And Do Something gives college scholarships.

TIP: *Middle schoolers are prime volunteer candidates because they are open to new experiences, and they are less likely than high school students to have calendars overstuffed with academics, extracurricular activities and a busy social life. They may be more inclined to want to sample a variety of experiences to see which ones they like best, so don't insist they make an ongoing commitment to one activity. To sample, they'll need to find nonprofits that can handle short-term or one-off volunteering.*

PROFILE IN GENEROSITY:

So Much to Do, So Hard to Choose

California ninth grader Alexandra Kukoff couldn't decide what charitable giving project she wanted to do for her bat mitzvah. She had so many causes she cared about that, if she tackled all of them, she'd never complete them before her coming-of-age ceremony. Then inspiration hit. She decided to write a book called A Jewish Girl's Guide to a Bat Mitzvah Project. *She interviewed women of all ages about the charitable projects they had undertaken, sharing the stories in a blog and on a Facebook page, where she also solicited other stories. By helping teens find projects, she inspired others to do charitable work, thus expanding the impact she alone could have.[3]*

---

[3] *"Teen Changemakers: An Interview with Teen Philanthropist Alexandra Kukoff" April 10, 2013, Jewish Communal Fund.*

Join the Club

Most kids love clubs. There's appeal in being part of something with structure, rules and expectations. Children also want to feel they belong. And there are lots of options for kids who want to help others and do so with friends. When I attended high school in a small Ohio town, one of the most important school organizations was the Service Over Self Club (SOS) for girls. (The boys could join our school's Key Club chapter—keyclub.org.) Any girl could belong as long as she committed to participating in the club's various service projects. It transcended the usual high school cliques. On meeting days, we all wore white blouses with an SOS monogram and our membership pins, and somehow this made us feel special when we walked down the halls.

Here are just a few examples of the many service clubs children can join today: Girl Scouts was founded with an emphasis on service, and even has a philanthropy merit badge along with many others in such "helping" skills as first aid. Religious congregations have long sponsored youth groups that stress service and stewardship. Newer on the scene are Girl Up clubs (girlup.org), sponsored by the United Nations Foundation (see Chapter 5), and Kids Care Clubs, sponsored by generationOn, the youth and family division of Points of Light. Kids Care Clubs (generationon.org/kids-care-clubs) are groups of elementary age children led by a parent or other adult facilitator, sometimes housed in a school or a faith-based group.

TIP: *In 2012, generationOn launched generationOn Service Clubs, similar to Kids Care Clubs but targeted to middle and high school-aged youth. The idea is that the kids choose and lead the club's service projects with the help of an adult advisor. Among the many resources provided at the website (generationon.org) are guides for family volunteering and for teens and advisors, mini-grants for projects, and stories about what clubs are doing.*

Although we typically think older kids—middle and high school age—prefer to volunteer with friends rather than their parents, I know a mom in California who joined a Mother-Daughter Philanthropy Club with her high school daughter. Club members volunteered for community projects and also held fundraisers. My friend said the club was not only a big help in the community, but it was a great way to help the moms and girls keep their relationships strong.

PROFILE IN GENEROSITY:

A Mother Starts a Movement

In 1990, Deborah Spaide and her husband wanted to introduce their five children to the benefits of helping others. They spent a day sprucing up the public housing apartment of an elderly woman who was extremely grateful. When the kids told their friends at school, they wanted to help, too. Spaide found it challenging to find nonprofit organizations that wanted youth volunteers but, with some creative thinking, she devised projects such as making bag lunches for a soup kitchen. Pretty soon, she had 50 kids in her group and a bunch of adults who wanted to know how to start a similar club. Thus, the Kids Care Clubs were born. Spaide created a newsletter, an organizing handbook and a website, and in 1995 published a well-received book called Teaching Your Kids to Care. *Today, the clubs are part of generationOn, (generationon.org/kids-care-clubs) the youth division of Points of Light, where you can find all the resources you need to start your own club.*

Seeking Money for Projects

When kids need money for their service projects, they typically hold a fundraiser (more on this in Chapter 4). But a growing number of organizations provide grants to encourage children to create volunteer projects. Disney, for example, in partnership with Youth Service America (YSA), offers Disney's Friends for Change Grants to help kids who are improving their communities' environment. The grants are available to schools, organizations and individuals planning service projects. The grants are for projects implemented by children ages 5 to 18. YSA offers other kinds of support for youth, including Summer of Service Awards. Do Something makes project grants, too.

TIP: *Family Volunteer Day, sponsored by Points of Light's generationOn, is held each year on the Saturday before Thanksgiving. The organization offers project grants and resource materials to support the day. Its website has a free downloadable guide with ideas for family-friendly projects (generationOn.org).*

Volunteer Vacations

Some families volunteer while on vacation. Dubbed philanthrotourism or voluntourism, these do-good trips typically last a week or more, depending on how much time and money the family can afford. You also can create a combination trip—a week repairing houses damaged by Hurricane Sandy, followed by some beach time on the Jersey shore, for example. Some families camp in and volunteer at state or national parks.

Volunteer trips are especially popular with high school and college students, and often involve travel abroad. Opportunities for families with younger children are more limited but growing. Global Citizens Network, for example, will work with families whose children are ages 8 and up, immersing them in other cultures ranging from a village in Kenya to an Indian Reservation in Washington State.

Volunteer vacations can be life-changing. Whether you go to Haiti to help build a school or to a national park to clear trails, you can learn a lot while bonding as a family. Such trips can also be challenging, both physically and emotionally, so they require careful planning. This includes figuring out what interests your kids, what kind of trip is appropriate for their ages, and then preparing them for what can be hard work and living conditions far different from what they are used to. If you are combining a volunteer experience with a vacation, some families suggest doing the fun part first. They say it can be disconcerting to spend a week working with families in poverty, then go off to a beach resort.

You can plan a trip on your own or find a local organization, such as a church or school that arranges service trips. Many people opt to work through a global organization that packages varieties of trips both domestically and abroad. There are a lot of tour operators, some better than others. Start by asking friends, neighbors or co-workers for recommendations, and search the Internet for "volunteer vacations for families" to find possibilities that fit your interests, age groups and budget. You typically have to provide your own transportation, pay for your own living expenses, and sometimes contribute to the program's operation.

If your high schooler is interested in a service trip, his or her school should have some resources to recommend. When you've located a few prospects, ask the organizations for references to families with kids of similar ages to yours who have already taken the trip. You'll want to inquire about safety, availability of medical facilities and the effectiveness of the program. Complaints have sometimes been raised about trip packagers who didn't have much meaningful work arranged for their volunteers or didn't provide opportunities for interaction with the local population as promised.

You don't have to spend a bunch of money to take a family volunteer vacation. Find a project near where you live and focus for a few days, or even just a weekend, on something other than your regular life.

TIP: *You can find more information at VolunTourism.org, which educates both travelers and organizations that arrange such travel.*

If you take a volunteer vacation, encourage your children to keep a journal during the trip. (Tell them they can turn it into a school report later.) Tweens and teens will probably want to post updates about their experiences on Facebook and Instagram, too. That assumes that they can connect to the Internet, not necessarily a given in some of the more remote parts of the U.S. and abroad.

Coaching When Kids Feel Discouraged

At some point during their volunteer experiences, your children may feel their individual efforts don't make enough of a difference in the face of so much need. Serving people in a soup kitchen or picking up trash in a stream bed can feel like tackling a problem that will never be solved. That's when a little motivational coaching can help.

They may not realize how much of an impact they are having, and how much individuals can accomplish by working together. For example, people at soup kitchens usually need more than a hot meal. Some feeding programs offer additional services that help people get back on their feet financially. But it's hard to improve your life if you are hungry, so providing meals is a critical first step.

Spark some conversation about attacking root causes. For instance, ask your kids how they could limit the trash from the stream bed. Maybe work to get more trash cans available, or post signs reminding people to carry away their trash to keep the stream clean for others. Kids often come up with brilliant solutions that present new volunteering opportunities.

PROFILE IN GENEROSITY:

The Story of the Starfish

Here's a popular story for when the job seems hopeless. (It has been retold in many versions by countless speakers, but the parable is thought to have originated with an essay by Loren Eiseley called "The Star Thrower," published in 1969.) The story goes like this: A young man is walking along the ocean and sees that thousands of starfish have washed ashore. Further along he sees an old man on the beach picking up one starfish at a time and throwing it back out to sea. "Why are you throwing starfish into the ocean?" the young man asks. "Because the sun is up, the tide is going out, and if I don't throw them further in, they will die," the old man replied. "But, old man, don't you realize there are miles and miles of beach and starfish all along it! You can't possibly save them all. You can't even save one tenth of them. In fact, even if you work all day, your efforts won't make any difference at all." The old man listened calmly, then bent down to pick up another starfish and threw it into the sea. "It made a difference to that one," he said.

CHAPTER 3:

Sharing Treasure

Unless someone like you cares a whole awful lot,
nothing is going to get better. It's not...

Dr. Seuss

Young people can donate money as well as time. Many children have income, either from an allowance or money they make from lawn work, babysitting and such. Some also fundraise for the causes they care about. Tell them that no donation is too small. Most charities find it especially rewarding to receive support from children, understanding that they might grow up to be adult supporters.

We believe kids should start getting an allowance around age 5 or 6—or as soon as they can differentiate between various denominations of money. (Do they know a dime is worth twice a nickel, regardless of which coin is larger?) Some parents require their children to divide the allowance into portions for sharing, spending and saving. Others just encourage their children to consider giving a portion to a good cause. Do what feels right for your family.

TIP: *In Chapter 6, we go into more detail about teaching kids about money and the ways to use an allowance as a valuable tool for raising financially literate children.*

The big challenge, for both children and adults, is deciding where to give. According to the National Center for Charitable Statistics, there are more than a million public charities registered in the United States. In addition, there are many people in need who might be helped directly. What's a donor to do?

Head and Heart Giving

Giving away money is a lot harder than it sounds. It would be easy to stand on a street corner and hand out dollar bills, but that wouldn't accomplish much for either the recipient or the giver. We all have limited amounts of time and money. Smart donors—even children—are thoughtful about which donations will have the most impact. That's the "head" part.

The "heart" is important, too. We want to give to a cause that aligns with our passions. If we love animals, then giving to the local animal shelter seems a no-brainer. But a wider look could turn up other deserving organizations as well: pet-fostering groups, companion-dog training programs and wild animal rescue sanctuaries, to name a few. Help your child weigh the organizations' results: how many pets are adopted compared with how many disabled people receive trained dogs compared with how many wild animals are nursed back to health. Children can be surprisingly thoughtful about where they think they'll do the most good if you help them frame the questions.

TIP: *Share with your children how you decide which charities you support. Do you give small gifts to a bunch of charities, or large gifts to just a few? What causes do you support and why? But don't push your favorites—let your children pick their own.*

Researching Charities

Most people don't research the performance of nonprofit organizations before they make a donation, according to a 2010 research report, called "Money for Good," by Hope Consulting. Instead, they give to organizations they already know well, such as their alma mater, religious congregation or a hospital where they have been treated. Young people, on the other hand, may decide first on something they care about and then find a related organization. You can help them learn how to do some homework first before donating.

If it's local, you might be able to visit the organization to see what happens there. (Being able to check out a charity first-hand is also a case for encouraging kids to fund locally, at least when they are younger, before they seek out national or global causes.) Animal shelters, for example, typically welcome visitors. Some organizations allow families to volunteer, which gives you insider knowledge of what the charity is accomplishing. Find out if the charity has a wish list. An animal shelter might need everything from blankets to pet food to cat toys. Wish lists sometimes specify what they don't want, too.

A charity's website is another go-to place. You can read—and sometimes watch videos—about the nonprofit's history, mission, services and goals. Nonprofits that are fully transparent will also post their board, staff, audited financial statements and tax filings. The website might list volunteer opportunities and other ways your family can get involved beyond giving money.

TIP: *Organizations must have 501(c)3 tax status from the Internal Revenue Service for your donation to be tax deductible. They have to file a Form 990 with the IRS each year, and some charities post the forms on their website. If they don't, you can ask the charity to send it to you. If they refuse, don't give them a donation.*

There are several Internet sites that report on nonprofit performance. At Guidestar's online database, you can search for an organization's most recent tax filing, which will list the charity's financials, leadership and other details. (Some basic information is available for free; more detailed data involves a fee.) Three leading sites that rate charities include the Better Business Bureau's Wise Giving Alliance, Charity Navigator and CharityWatch (requires a membership donation). Two caveats: you won't find all nonprofits on these rating sites, and there has been some criticism over the criteria they use to assess performance.

Handling Panhandlers

Especially when children are young, they like to give spontaneously. And parents hate to tamp down a generous impulse. A common dilemma is how to handle panhandlers who approach you and your children on the street. It's hard to explain to the very young that giving money may not be helpful if it's used to feed an alcohol or drug addiction. If you live in an urban area, you'll likely run into this frequently, so it's good to have a consistent message. One approach is to give food, by offering to buy the person a sandwich, for example. Some families carry around gift cards in small denominations for fast food restaurants.

Another alternative is to explain to your children that you don't give money to individuals on the street because you'd rather support organizations that help people in need with more than just a meal. In either case, you should model compassion by being polite, not hostile, to panhandlers, even if you aren't going to give them a handout. Also, talk to your children about the variety of circumstances that can cause people to be poor or homeless through no fault of their own.

TIP: *Many cities have "street newspapers" that employ the homeless and inform readers about the issue. The DC version is* Street Sense, *and we always buy it when we see a vendor because we know that person is earning a living from the sales. The newspaper also gives vendors a voice, since half the content—news, features, poems, and so forth—is written by homeless or formerly homeless residents. If your city has one, buy it and read it with your children.*

When It Is Someone Else's Favorite Charity

Adults often feel obligated to give to charities that don't really interest them. Friends ask you to buy a ticket to a fundraiser or a chance on a door prize, or to sponsor them in a walk-a-thon. Children receive such requests, too, especially teens active on social media, a hot-bed of fundraising. Brainstorm with your children about ways to handle this.

Sometimes a friend's recommendation will introduce your son or daughter to a charity they, too, will become passionate about. Other times, they'll have to say no because there is a limit to what they can give to. It's easy to avoid on social media by just not responding to every pitch. Instead of contributing, your kids might opt to share the information about the cause with their networks. Personal requests require a more personal response. You might want to say "yes" to a close friend who seeks support for something she really cares about. For others, kids can be honest and say "I only have a limited amount that I can give to charity, and I'm supporting my own favorites right now."

Honoring someone else can be a great way to give. A mother I met told me her children had pooled their money one Christmas to make a donation to their grandparents' favorite charity in their names. She said her parents were incredibly moved. "I'd never seen my dad get teary before," she explained.

Sources of Money for Donations

Besides their allowances, children sometimes receive large cash gifts to mark milestones: significant birthdays, graduations and so forth. Any time your children receive gifts of cash, encourage them to donate a portion to a cause they care about.

Gift-giving occasions, such as Christmas, Hanukkah and birthdays, can also be occasions to include the gift of giving—a small amount of money your children can donate to their favorite charities. Younger ones may require help identifying a charity, while older ones can do their own research. You'll still likely need to use your credit card to make the transaction if your children donate online. You could also suggest this gift idea to the grandparents. Amounts don't have to be large. One grandmother we know who lives far away from her six grandchildren sent each one $25 at Thanksgiving, explaining that they should show their gratitude for what they have by giving a gift to a worthy organization. She asked them each to write her a letter explaining who they gave the money to and why. She was overwhelmed by the heartfelt answers she got back. The oldest sent hers to a breast cancer charity because her mother is a survivor. The youngest gave his to the animal shelter where their family had adopted kittens "so more animals can have homes."

Charity Cards

Some parents buy charity gift cards for children to use to make donations, but the cards have drawbacks. *Consumer Reports* cautions that gift cards come with fees and sometimes with expiration dates. Some don't give the designated charity the contribution for months while earning interest on the money. Critics suggest you give the money straight to the charity and avoid the middle man. Supporters say the cards are convenient for the recipient who can choose how to direct the gift. If you decide to go the card route, do an Internet search on "Charity Gift Cards" to see what's out there and compare the costs and ease of use.

TIP: *One popular site for gift cards is Razoo.com, which also is a crowd-funding site where you can create your own fundraising campaign for a cause.*

Fundraising Projects

Most of us tried the classic lemonade stand when we were kids. It's about as simple as a fundraiser can get, and it's especially suitable for younger children. They learn about publicity, customer service and making change. If the funds raised are going to charity rather than into the child's pocket, customers are more enthusiastic. Right after Hurricane Katrina, I went to our neighborhood farmers market and saw kids in front of a house across the street selling lemonade to raise money to help the victims. They were doing a huge business.

When they get older, most young people gravitate to fundraising with friends. Car washes remain a perennial favorite, but kids can be very creative with ideas. Also popular are the charity walks/runs/bike rides where participants solicit sponsors to donate based on the distance traveled. The digital world has added a new dimension to old-school fundraising. It's much easier to reach friends to be fundraiser donors or walk-a-thon sponsors using social media.

TIP: *Offer to match all or a portion of the money your children raise. This shows you applaud their efforts. If your company has a matching gifts program, you could also get a match for a charity you and your child support.*

Regulations? Really?

It may sound crazy, but some lemonade stands, car washes and other fundraisers occasionally run afoul of local regulations. Some kids in our area set up a charity lemonade stand near the entrance to a big golf tournament and were shut down by county enforcement officers because they didn't have a vendor's license and were too close to the main entrance where traffic and safety were a concern. The county relented after the families agreed to help their kids move farther from the entrance.

In 2014, Arlington County, Virginia, banned kids' charity car washes. Reason: The county is subject to new storm-water regulations that could be undermined by large amounts of detergents and other pollutants flowing into storm drains and threatening the Chesapeake Bay. In a letter to middle and high school students, school officials suggested they try environmentally friendly fundraisers instead, like selling reusable water bottles.

PROFILE IN GENEROSITY:

Alex's Lemonade Stands

Alexandra "Alex" Scott started battling brain cancer before she was 1-year-old. In 2000, when she was 4, she announced that she wanted to open a lemonade stand to raise money to help doctors find a cure for all children with cancer. The first stand raised $2,000 for pediatric cancer research, and the family held the sale annually after that. News spread around the world and, by the time Alex died at age 8, lemonade stands in her name had raised $1 million and became the inspiration for a national movement led by the Alex's Lemonade Stand Foundation. National Lemonade Days are a three-day event in June when kids and families across the country collectively raise more than $1 million. That's a lot of cups of lemonade!

TIP: *Go to Alexslemonade.org for tips on how to run a lemonade stand as well as other types of fundraisers. You can also register at the site and send the foundation money that your children raise.*

Charity Birthday Parties

Some kids' birthday parties smack of wretched excess with all the presents even very young children receive. As a result, there's a trend toward charity birthday parties. In lieu of gifts, kids invite their friends to bring something to donate for a cause of the birthday child's choosing: children's books for a literacy program, pet food for an animal rescue group, school supplies for a family shelter, or even cash for a favorite charity. You can even build a service component into the party, such as assembling activity boxes for hospitalized children, writing greeting cards for overseas military personnel, or making dog biscuits for the animal shelter.

Charity birthday parties are not without critics. Some people think kids should be allowed to have gifts on their birthday, period. I think the children should decide if they want to make their party a charity event.

More kids will choose this option if they:

- pick the charity themselves;
- can see the results—such as delivering donated goods to a nonprofit;
- receive a few presents from their family outside of the party.

Shopping for Good

Tons of businesses foster a good image by donating a portion of their profits to charity. With a few exceptions, I feel that companies can do good without making me buy their products. But you can teach your children to shop and do good simultaneously by buying from nonprofits.

If your children need birthday gifts for friends, for instance, you can take them to the gift shop at your local zoo, children's museum or science center. If they need some summer reading, shop the used book sales that are frequently held by library friends' groups. Check out online catalogues, too. The Sesame Street Store has great gifts for the younger set, and the proceeds help the nonprofit Sesame Workshop produce shows for children in 120 countries. Your children also can buy cards and gifts from UNICEF (unicefusa.org).

Some teens shop for gifts at Goodwill or other charity thrift stores because they not only get things cheap, but also help others served by the nonprofit and keep unwanted items out of landfills. A triple bottom line! Many faith-based organizations sponsor alternative gift markets at Christmas where you can make donations in the name of someone else. Our church has one called Gifts of Hope, and it's so much fun to see families going from table to table checking out the options and discussing whether Grandma would like to receive a donation in her name to buy a flock of chickens for Heifer, a Christmas dinner for a needy family or a partial scholarship at a mission school in Kenya. Every donation comes with a gift card to send to the one honored. Check your community news sources or inquire on your neighborhood listserv to find an alternative gifts market in your area.

 Digital Deed: **Amazon, through its Amazon Smile program, donates 0.5 percent of the price of your families' eligible purchases to the charitable organization of your choice. It won't add up to big bucks unless you do a lot of online shopping. But, as long as you are spending money there anyway, you might as well do some good. Let your kids help you pick the charity. Sign up at smile.amazon.com.**

PROFILE IN GENEROSITY:

Chickens or a Goat?

Heifer International has long been a favorite of ours. From Heifer's catalogue, families can "buy" an animal to help a family in another part of the world and read about how that animal will help end poverty. The year I taught a Sunday School class, the kids decided to pool their offerings that Christmas to fund a Heifer animal. Great plan, I thought. What I hadn't expected was their lengthy—and at times heated—debate about which animal to buy. It got down to a flock of chickens versus a portion of a goat. I was surprised at how thoughtfully these 9-year-olds considered which gift would have the most impact.

TIP: *At Heifer's website (heifer.org), you'll find examples of anti-poverty fundraising projects run by schools, religious congregations and individual children.*

The Dinner Table Foundation

In *The Giving Family: Raising Our Children to Help Others*, I described the Dinner Table Foundation. It wasn't an original idea; I knew families that were already doing it. But it's one of the activities I get asked about most often.

The concept is simple but can have many variations. Basically, a family gathers around a table for a family meeting. The purpose is to make decisions together about how to allocate an amount of money for charity. Some families do this annually at Thanksgiving or during the December holidays; others set a date quarterly. Usually the parents provide the pot of money, but sometimes older kids are expected to chip in. Some families include grandparents in the meeting.

To get started, especially with young children, parents guide the discussion by passing around appeals from organizations that have particular interest to their children—an animal shelter, a sports program serving low income kids, the local children's hospital, a food bank or a zoo, for example. When kids are older, they can research groups online and bring their own ideas to the table.

Families can make these decisions in a variety of ways. Some allow each child to allocate a certain amount. Others require the kids to reach consensus on one or two charities. Pick a method that seems best for your family and be open to making changes as you gain experience.

PROFILE IN GENEROSITY:

The Family Meeting

Not all kids will take to family activities such as the dinner table foundation with the same enthusiasm. Some gentle probing may reveal the reasons and possible solutions. Our friend Karen tried the family meeting idea and got off to a rough start. It was obvious that her youngest son, then around 7, just wasn't comfortable being there. He fidgeted, didn't participate and generally made his discomfort clear from his body language. Finally, Karen had a chat with him about why he didn't like the family meetings. "I don't know what to expect," he replied. Further questions revealed what he meant. In school they had morning meetings, and his teacher always wrote on a white board an agenda of three to four discussion items listed and numbered. Then he knew what to expect and could follow along. At the next meeting, Karen pulled an easel up to the table and wrote an agenda. That one small change made her son a happy participant in the discussions.

TIP: *If you want to expand your group effort, consider starting a giving circle with other families or create one for your children and their friends. See Chapter 9 to learn how to start and run a giving circle, or to find out about youth grantmaking groups and other kinds of cooperative giving.*

Too Much of a Good Thing?

Have you done your job so well that now your son or daughter wants to give away the store? If buying one bag of canned goods for the food bank feels so good, why not buy 10, they wonder? Both an individual child and a family have to make decisions about what portion of their funds they'll allocate to charity. Finding a way to balance generosity with other needs and wants is part of a child's giving education. And it's a good lesson in budgeting, too. An allowance is a tool that helps you teach this.

It gets trickier when the child just wants to give away the family's money without kicking in some of his own. Generosity can be part of that message, too. Avoid conveying the message that philanthropy is just about giving away other people's money.

Donate Non-Cash Treasure

The mantra "Reduce, Reuse, Recycle" is one every child should learn. It's better for our environment if we don't accumulate so much stuff. Plus we don't waste money on things we don't really need, and we responsibly dispose of what we do own. If we have things that we no longer need but someone else can put to good use, we help others and the environment when we give those things away.

 **Digital Deed:** **Many communities have Freecycle groups. This online service, run by volunteers, lets you post things you don't want and connect with people who do and are willing to pick them up. Our family has found new homes for many items this way. Families frequently offer outgrown jigsaw puzzles, games, toys, baby equipment and even school supplies. Check freecycle.org to find out if they serve your local area.**

Your children can help research where your gently-used items can go. You'd be surprised at the array of things charities need. Julie even donated her wedding gown to a nonprofit that resells dresses to raise funds for breast cancer outreach and education.

Here are some more ideas:

- Some high schools run drives to collect prom dresses, shoes and accessories and set up free shops for girls who can't afford to buy their own.

- Sports leagues collect outgrown sports equipment, such as soccer shoes and shin guards, to pass on to others.

- The Lions Club collects used eyeglasses and refurbishes them to help children and adults around the world. Check their website to locate the collection boxes in your area. You can also mail glasses to them.

- Cell phones, computers and other electronics can be donated to charities that will refurbish them for people in need.

TIP: *Many airlines let you donate frequent flier miles to charity. Some of the big recipients include the Make a Wish Foundation, to fly ill children and their families to wish destinations, and the American Red Cross, which flies volunteers to disaster scenes. Search your airline's frequent flier program page for a list of donation options, and let your kids help you choose where to donate the miles.*

PROFILE IN GENEROSITY:

Hanukkah Tradition

Jen Bokoff, director of GrantCraft, a service of the Foundation Center, a resource for funders, describes her family's informal giving circle this way: "My family began a tradition when my cousins and I were young, where every Hanukkah, each family member individually recommends a charitable cause for a group donation. In making the recommendation, each person shares a bit about why they like the program or organization. We ultimately draw one out of a hat, and this selection becomes an organization that we all give to and learn more about that year. In our yearly giving circle, we see evidence of shared values with gifts and repetition across generations. But especially as the cousins have gotten older, there has been a shift towards discussing needs and merits of specific programs rather than just supporting the overall mission." (From GrantCraft's Sept. 11, 2013 blog, used with permission.)

CHAPTER 4:

The Digital Philanthropist

We do not need magic to change the world; we carry all the power we need inside ourselves already: We have the power to imagine better...

Author J.K. Rowling

In the sculpture garden of the National Gallery of Art in Washington, DC, there's a sculpture that appears to be a disk topped by a bundle of long brush bristles. On a visit there with Julie when she was about 14, she asked me what it was. "It's supposed to look like a typewriter eraser," I explained. She looked so baffled, I half expected her to ask "What's a typewriter?" She got her own, simple computer for Christmas when she was 6, so I wouldn't have to share the one I used for my freelance writing business. Later, she became a pro at surfing the Internet. She is a Digital Native and part of the Always On generation.

When I was growing up, my knowledge of human needs was largely local—in my small town, Circleville, Ohio. My mother was in charge of the food stamp program at the county welfare department, so I had plenty of perspective on hunger and need. My Millennial daughter's childhood awareness was global. It was hard for her to ignore images of starving refugees in war-torn countries on the other side of the world and not want to do something.

Almost at the speed of light, kids have gone from desktop computers, to laptops to tablets, and now, mostly mobile phones for their connectivity. To say there has been an explosion in the use of social media is a huge understatement. And there is constant change. Adults are finding that kids don't answer emails or phone calls; they prefer to text. Many teens are shifting from Facebook, using Twitter and Instagram instead. By the time you read this, the popular methods of communication will probably have shifted again.

Members of Generation Z (the cohort that follows the Millennials and is generally pegged as having birth years starting around 2000 and continuing to present day) are practically born with smartphones in their hands. Who hasn't seen a harried parent give her smartphone or tablet to a toddler to keep him occupied? My Little Pony or a Batman action figure can't compete with the flashing lights and colors of an online game. Much has been said and written about the effects, both negative and positive, of technology on children. Our position is that kids using technology is now a fact of life. Used wisely, it can be a powerful tool to help children with their philanthropy.

Aria Finger, Chief Operating Officer of Do Something, said the new online world children live in "is not a bad thing. It's just different and new. We have to accept that it's part of our ecosystem, then figure out how to use it for good." She cited the example of one of Do Something's many campaigns, Birthday Mail, through which young people send birthday cards to homeless children. "Often, teens do it alone, and sometimes they do it with friends at their house. But then they go online and get excited to see thousands of others doing it. That's important."

Where Do You Come In?

Because of technology, parents often are no longer the middlemen for their older children's giving. On their own, some young people are texting donations to the Red Cross during disasters, finding causes through their friends' or their favorite celebrity's tweets, and locating volunteer opportunities—locally and abroad—through Facebook and other social media. They fund classroom needs through DonorsChoose.org, make microloans overseas through Kiva.org and create YouTube videos promoting their favorite causes. But parents still have a role to play in helping their children navigate this new philanthropy landscape, find their passions and experience real world—not just virtual—giving.

Parents should mainly facilitate, not direct. By asking questions, you can help your children surface their passions so they can narrow in on sites that address those interests. You can also help them develop their critical sensibilities so they know how to assess what they are getting involved in.

 **Digital Deed:** Here's an example of an online resource to make kindness contagious. A friend introduced me to Smile Cards, available from Kindspring, a volunteer-run nonprofit. At this website, www.kindspring.org, children can get ideas for acts of kindness and also download free, printable cards (or buy a set of preprinted glossy ones). The instructions are to:

1. Do an act of kindness.

2. Leave a "smile card" to encourage the recipient to pay the kindness forward.

3. Share your experience on the website.

4. Change the world one small act at a time.

Online vs. Hands-on Philanthropy

A widely held assumption that young people who spend a lot of time using social media won't spend time volunteering doesn't hold up. Research by Do Something, for example, found that young people who report sending many text messages were 13 percent more likely to have volunteered in the last year than those who had mobile phones but didn't text regularly, and they were 38 percent more likely to volunteer than those without phones. The research also found young people were 66 percent more likely to find volunteer activities by talking to people than from online sources.

Digital philanthropy is not a substitute, but it can be a powerful tool for giving and serving. Parents can help by talking to their children about how to have the biggest impact with online tools. The Internet expands a child's community to include the whole world. But a simple act like texting $10 to earthquake victims in another country might not be very meaningful unless parents encourage their children to go deeper.

"The conversation your children have with you about it is as important as the action they take," said Jenny Friedman, founder of Doing Good Together. Instead of a young person making a loan through Kiva "and checking it off the list, ask 'What do you think will happen with this loan? How do you think it will help the family?'" Then brainstorm what else they can do.

Talking about ways to help others by using online tools can bring families closer together, Friedman added. "Parents think if we don't have the right answer, we shouldn't have the conversation. Social problems are enormous. You can explain why you are ambivalent about supporting a particular cause or about mistakes you've made as a giver, as you help kids find the things they want to support. Show respect for them, and they'll start coming up with ideas."

A donation to an overseas nonprofit can spark questions "about how we can be effective in international communities we are not a part of and not be condescending," Friedman said. "How do we avoid thinking we can go in and solve other people's problems?" Such questions enable parents to put digital philanthropy in context for their children.

The Cult of Celebrity

Have your children texted a donation to an organization based solely on a tweet from their favorite celebrity? Aria Finger advises parents not to get too judgmental about the passions their children pursue, even those of a favorite celeb, because anything that engages young people in giving is a good thing and can lead them to more good works. For example, superstar Justin Bieber, despite several recent run-ins with the law, still has the second highest number of Twitter followers as of this writing. When he urged his millions of fans on social media to support his favorite cause, Pencils of Promise (PoP), he drove countless youths to the organization's website. Many donated to help the organization build and equip schools in developing countries where children lack access to a quality education. Started by a young man named Adam Braun, PoP has been described as a "movement of students for students."

As Braun explains on the organization's website, PoP began when he was backpacking in India and asked a boy, who was begging, "What do you want most in the world? The answer was 'A pencil.' I reached into my backpack, handed him my pencil, and watched as a wave of possibility washed over him. Over the next five years I backpacked through more than 50 countries, handing out thousands of pens and pencils across six continents."

TIP: *The Pencils of Promise website (pencilsofpromise.org) is a good example of one that is kid-friendly. It explains in very simple terms—and with lots of visuals—the challenge the organization is addressing, its impact, and specific ways people can help by donating both money and time through social media campaigns.*

Favorite books and movies also inspire children and teens. The Harry Potter Alliance (www.hpalliance.org), for example, is a nonprofit that uses parallels in the Harry Potter books to educate and mobilize young people to address issues such as inequality, illiteracy and human rights violations. The website shows kids how to create alliance chapters and undertake projects in their communities. The success of this effort led the organization to create the Imagine Better Project, which brings together fans of other books, TV shows, movies and YouTube celebrities to harness pop culture as a way to make civic engagement exciting and to mobilize young people to change the world.

Using Technology to Give, to Serve, to Act

Here's a sampling of the ways children can use online tools to give:

Digital Fundraising

Let's say your child is concerned about childhood hunger. A generation ago, she might have organized a bake sale and sent the proceeds off to a food pantry. Today, the Internet can take a bake sale to a whole new level. No Kids Hungry, a project of Share Our Strength, has a website where children can:

- Learn about the problem of childhood hunger.
- See videos of other kids' success with bake sales and post their own.
- Start their own sale or connect with one already scheduled in their area.
- Get tons of tips about successful sales, including recipes.
- Download posters and other promotional material.
- Involve others through their social media network.
- Learn how the donations are used and the impact they have.

This is typical of many sites that children are using today to make a difference. They help kids learn about the problem, actions they can take and how the donations are used.

PROFILE IN GENEROSITY:

A Girl's Dream of Clean Water

*One of the most inspiring—and heart-breaking—stories I ever heard
was about Rachel Beckwith. The Seattle girl was only 8 when her
church started raising money to build wells in Africa. Shocked to learn
about the millions of children and adults who lack clean water, Rachel
decided to forgo gifts for her ninth birthday and asked friends and
family to donate $9 to a fundraising page she set up on the website of
an organization called "charity: water" (charitywater.org). Her goal was
to raise $300, but she was disappointed when she was $80 short by her
birthday on June 12, 2011. A few weeks later, Rachel was riding with
her family on an interstate when two trucks collided, causing a multi-
vehicle pile-up. Although the rest of the family escaped unharmed, she
was critically injured, and died on July 23. The family donated her
organs as well as her hair. Rachel had already donated her hair to Locks
for Love twice before so she could help sick children.*

*Word spread on social media about Rachel's story, and soon
people all over the world were donating to her webpage. The donations
eventually exceeded $1 million, and funded water projects in many
communities across Ethiopia. On the one-year anniversary of Rachel's
death, her mother Samantha Paul and her grandparents went to
Ethiopia to view some of Rachel's water projects and to meet the
villagers who benefited. Rachel's memory is kept alive there by the
people who know their clean water was made possible by the generous
example of a young girl from the United States who had never been to
Africa but who wanted to help other children in need.*

Virtual Volunteering

More nonprofits are getting savvy about using volunteers who prefer to work online and on their own schedules. Some organizations even have online jobs that just take a few minutes, called micro-volunteering. Your children may be able to find virtual volunteering jobs on the website of an organization they are interested in by clicking on a tab called "How You Can Help" or "Volunteering."

They might be asked to upload images, tag photos, write for a blog or advocate for a cause through social media. The National Archives, for example, has a virtual volunteer program called Citizen Archivist. They have tons of fascinating images waiting to be tagged so other researchers can find them. Some projects specify they are appropriate for beginners. A teenage history or science buff might enjoy transcribing old ships' logs to get historical weather data used for climate model projections. In 2014, the Smithsonian launched a Transcription Center to crowd-source the digitization of documents such as old diaries.

TIP: *Volunteermatch.org not only is an excellent source for volunteer jobs in your community, including ones for young people, it also lets you search for virtual jobs.*

Playing Games

Most school-age kids play video games—some occasionally, some excessively. The violent ones have given such games a bad name, but researchers say that some online games can help kids learn to solve problems and collaborate. Now we are seeing more games designed to address social issues. In some cases, the games themselves raise money for a cause.

Games for Change is leading the charge by facilitating the creation of social impact games that leverage entertainment for social good. At the website gamesforchange.org, there are free games suitable for kids 7 and up to try and even rate.

Crowd-funding

Sites like DonorsChoose.org, which link donors with teachers in economically challenged schools, are popular with young donors because they can relate to classroom needs and quickly see a project funded. Julie's former college roommate Beth was a Teach for America science teacher at a low-income middle school in North Carolina. Frustrated by the dryness of the standard textbook, which was beyond many of her students' reading levels, she created a $150 Donors Choose project to buy supplemental books. Her project was funded in just a few days. It worked so well that Beth used the site again the following year when she decided to start a school choir and needed to buy music-arranging software; her friends and family came through once again. Children who like the idea of funding classroom projects can go directly to the site and search by type of project, age group, location, etc., to find something that appeals to them.

Digital Deed: **A number of nonprofits offer "click to give" options. FreeRice.com, for example, is a popular trivia game for kids and adults. Each correct answer earns a donation of 10 grains of rice through the United Nations World Food Program. The donations are generated through sponsor ads, and, since the game's founding in 2007, game players have fed millions of people. You can start with vocabulary questions and move on to other subjects. It's a way to have fun, learn and make a difference.**

Microfinance: A Ticket Out of Poverty

Nobel Peace Prize winner Muhammad Yunus, founder of the Grameen Bank in Bangladesh, pioneered the idea of making very small loans to poor people—mainly women—so they could start or expand a business and lift themselves out of poverty. He had no idea how widely the concept would spread within two decades.

Today it's easy for families to participate in micro-lending through sites such as Kiva (kiva.org). Praised by former President Bill Clinton in his book *Giving: How Each of Us Can Change the World* (Knopf, 2007), and endorsed by Oprah Winfrey, Kiva lets you make loans as small as $25 to help poor people around the world start and grow businesses, build homes, go to school, or switch to solar energy, among many examples. A network of field partners in the various countries vet and disperse the loans. The lender gets regular updates on how the borrower is doing, and once the loan is paid off, the lender can loan it again to a new borrower. The site displays pictures and tells the story of each prospective borrower. For example, a woman in a developing country needs $350 to purchase materials to make rugs for sale. Individual loans through Kiva are pooled to equal that amount. As she sells her goods, she pays back the loan in small installments. It's a type of crowd-funding, but since it's only a loan, you can keep reinvesting the same amount of money.

TIP: *Kiva has teamed up with Citi to create Kiva U, a project to form clubs in schools and colleges so young people can engage together in changing the world through micro-lending (kiva.org/kivau).*

Digital Activism

The digital world offers young people a much wider platform than we Boomers had to advocate for causes. A popular example is Change.org, a website that has been successfully used by countless kids and adults to press for change. Here's a favorite example: When the movie version of Dr. Seuss's book *The Lorax* came out, a fourth grade class in Brooklyn didn't like the trailer for the film because it totally missed the story's environmental message. Their teacher helped them start a petition on Change.org that collected thousands of signatures and led Universal Pictures to beef up the film's website to include educational materials about trees and what young people can do to help save the environment.

Give the Gift of Stories

Technology offers cool new ways to preserve memories. Using an app called Sound Cloud (free for iOS and Android), you can record a loved one's story and upload it to StoryCorps, a national effort to record the stories of ordinary people—one of the nation's largest oral history projects. The website storycorps.org has a step-by-step guide, including tips on making audio recordings and sample questions to ask. All StoryCorps interviews are archived at the American Folklife Center at the Library of Congress. These recordings become treasured heirlooms in families and can be played at reunions and other gatherings. This is also a great way for young people to connect to elders or seniors in nursing homes. There's even a StoryCorps initiative—with separate how-to guide—for people with memory loss, who often feel isolated but still have amazing stories to share with future generations.

#GivingTuesday™

First there was Thanksgiving, but then came the shopping frenzy dubbed Black Friday (which now starts on Thursday!). Then it's on to Cyber Monday with more frantic spending. It was all too much for New York City's 92nd Street Y, which in 2012, started a new day—Giving Tuesday. In partnership with the United Nations Foundation, the Y recruited philanthropy leaders, corporate partners and lots of nonprofits, to promote the idea of a day devoted to giving as an apt start to the holiday season. Now the day's name has been trademarked with a hash tag to emphasize the social media aspects of the campaign, and that seemingly simple idea has launched a movement.

The first year, the initiative attracted more than 2,600 partners, from local nonprofits to multinational corporations from all 50 states and DC. They were either registered charities with a specific project, or they were businesses, schools, religious or community groups that committed to spearhead a project benefiting at least one nonprofit. This was an amazing feat given that the event held on Nov. 27 had launched less than three months earlier in September. Many nonprofits saw their online giving jump by record amounts. Some groups used the day as an opportunity to engage volunteers in projects. Since then, the growth is nothing short of phenomenal. In 2013, the $20 million donated was 90 percent higher than the previous year, and 10,000 charities, companies and others participated.

Writing on the *Harvard Business Review* blog about the first year, co-founder Henry Timms from the Y said: "The community that got behind #GivingTuesday grew beyond our highest expectations…The campaign was endorsed by the White House and Bill Gates, generated more than 800 media features and mentions in outlets like CNN, the *Washington Post* and CBS News, and our hash tag trended No. 1 on Twitter."

With such success, it was obvious that it would become a permanent fixture on our calendars and in our mindset. It's easy for kids to get involved. And it's much better to make donations at the beginning of the holiday season than at the end when we are tapped out.

Digital Deed: The #GivingTuesday™ website has ideas for ways families can support their favorite nonprofits through donations of volunteer time and money. There's also a section on how to be a Social Media Ambassador to spread the word to others.

Safety in Cyberspace

While safety online is beyond the scope of this book, every parent needs to know about it. The Federal Trade Commission is responsible for enforcing the Children's Online Privacy Protections Act (COPPA) designed to secure the privacy and safety of children under age 13. At ftc.org you can download a guide called "Net Cetera: Chatting With Kids About Being Online." Also, the nonprofit Common Sense Media is a good source for information, including ratings of movies, games, websites and apps. Sign up for their helpful blog for parents.

PROFILE IN GENEROSITY:

Melinda Gates on Social Media

Speaking to the Duke University graduating class of 2013, Melinda Gates, co-chair of the Bill & Melinda Gates Foundation, noted that the Millennial generation gets branded as being more focused on connecting online than in person.

"The way you communicate is the single biggest difference between you now and me a generation ago," she told the graduates. Smartphones and other technologies have proliferated, even in a Kenyan slum she had recently visited, making it possible for Americans to get to know people in other countries more personally. "Your world really can become a neighborhood," Gates said, contending that "deep human connection... is not a tool. It's not a means to an end. It is the end—the purpose and the result of a meaningful life—and it will inspire the most amazing acts of love, generosity and humanity."

CHAPTER 5:

Pick a Cause, Any Cause

How lovely to think that no one need wait a moment; we can start now, start slowly changing the world!

Anne Frank (diary entry, 1944)

It has taken me most of my adult life to learn to say no. I've learned the hard way that just because someone asks me to volunteer for a project doesn't mean that I have the needed skill set or adequate time or even any interest. My inborn guilt has kept me in volunteer jobs way past the time when I should have pulled the plug because my heart just wasn't in it. And who among us hasn't donated to a cause that we didn't really care much about just because we felt obligated when friends asked us to? And will they feel the same way when we in turn ask them to contribute to one of our favorite nonprofits?

The same thing can happen to children. A friend asks them to support a cause or a parent promotes a particular project or their school lines up a community service activity expecting everyone to gladly join in. But this is not a formula for keeping a young person engaged. The most avid volunteers and givers figure out their passions, then find the projects that fit both their hearts and their heads.

Here's how you can help. Children usually have many interests and skills. But they often need someone to recognize and point out what they have to contribute and what kinds of projects fits those attributes. Is your son or daughter a singer/dancer/musician? Nursing homes are always looking for free entertainment for residents. Is she a dedicated athlete? She can organize a drive to collect gently used equipment or funds for registration fees for kids from families that can't afford them. Or she can volunteer to coach a team for younger children or help with a Special Olympics event. Children who are avid readers can hold book drives to benefit schools with limited libraries, or they can read to younger ones. Computer whizzes can teach senior citizens to use social media. A teen who's good in math could tutor youngsters in a neighborhood after-school program. The ideas are endless. It just takes some brainstorming with someone who may know them better than they know themselves.

It's also good to go with what they know. Personal connections are often the basis of the most rewarding giving opportunities. Tweens and teens can ask about volunteer jobs in places they enjoy—the library, a playground, a sports program, their former after-school program or nursery school, summer camps—anywhere they've spent some pleasant hours. Those memories can motivate them to give back so others can have that same experience.

Difficult times can spur a child's interests, too. Plenty of young people have participated in cancer charity fundraising after a relative had cancer. A child who has been hospitalized, and knows how boring the days can be, might enjoy putting together and delivering activities kits for young patients. I read about a high-schooler who was treated for a rare tumor and, while she recuperated at home from surgery, she made jewelry to keep busy. Then she sold it and donated half the proceeds to the hospital that treated her.

PROFILE IN GENEROSITY:

The Jester Has Lost His Jingle

A few years ago, I had the pleasure of meeting Barbara Saltzman, whose son David died of cancer in 1990 at age 22. For his senior project at Yale, while he was undergoing treatment, David wrote and illustrated The Jester Has Lost His Jingle. *His family promised him they'd get it published, and today this award-winning book and Jester dolls have been distributed to thousands of children in hospitals to help them cope with illness, especially cancer. The book's whimsical story told in rhyme describes the adventures of an optimistic Jester and his puppet pal Pharley. The message of laughter and hope has provided emotional support to countless children and their families.*

School kids can get involved by holding read-a-thons to earn money to donate copies of the book and doll to their local hospital. This and other programs are run by The Jester and Pharley Phund, a nonprofit Barbara started to expand the book's reach. Teachers report the read-a-thons help their students become better readers while also teaching them about helping others. If your kids would like to take on this project, go to thejester.org.

TIP: *As children get older and discover more about the world, their interests usually change, sometimes frequently. It's not uncommon, for example, for a child to be passionate about animals, and later develop more of an interest in the environment. Be alert to such changes and share news articles or website links when you see projects that might excite them. Otherwise, they could end up simply following what their friends do instead of finding projects they will truly love.*

In Chapter 2, we covered donating time and, in Chapter 3, donating or raising money. In this chapter, we've grouped projects in categories based on a child's interests or passions. We've included ideas to fit kids of all ages, and all of these projects can use time *and* money.

Animals

Many children, especially younger ones, care deeply about animals. Regardless of whether they have pets themselves, they can find lots of ways to help animals and have fun doing it. Here are some popular projects:

- Offer to walk an elderly neighbor's dog.
- Help care for the pets of someone who is sick.
- Volunteer to take home and care for the class pet during school vacations.
- "Adopt an animal" at the local zoo.
- Foster dogs, cats, even guinea pigs for a rescue organization.
- Bake dog biscuits to donate to shelters.

TIP: *An animal loving child might like to have a pet-themed birthday party and ask guests to bring something from the local animal shelter's wish list instead of a gift for the host. (Provide suggestions in the invitations.) Delivering the gifts to the shelter could even be a party activity.*

Animal Shelters Have Many Opportunities to Give

Shelters need all kinds of help. Many need volunteers to walk dogs or play with cats, rabbits or other animals. Although they typically require volunteers to be 18 or older, many have junior volunteer programs where a child as young as 12 or so can volunteer as long as he or she is accompanied by a parent or guardian who is responsible for the animal handling. Some shelters require a minimum time commitment; for example, eight hours a month for six months plus a training course. Check this out before your child gets enthusiastic and you find the commitment is too much for your own schedule.

TIP: *Go to shelterproject.org to search by zip code for an animal shelter or rescue group in your neighborhood. Then visit that shelter's site to learn how to help.*

Some shelters post wish lists on their websites for everything from toys and treats to blankets and kitty litter. Another option is to foster an animal by providing a temporary home until the pet is adopted. This helps a homeless pet and also frees up space in the shelter for other abandoned animals.

From Julie

After college, I volunteered at the Maryland SPCA in Baltimore once a week, walking dogs and playing with cats. Among the many things I learned: Not all dogs like to play fetch—who knew?—but they pretty much all like having their bellies rubbed. And I learned that kids can be incredibly generous with their time and money. Although safety concerns meant that volunteers working directly with animals had to be 17, much younger kids found ways to contribute. We often had children who had asked for gifts for the shelter animals instead of birthday presents. Their parents would roll in with a trunk-load full of rawhide bones for the dogs and toy mice for the cats. (You can imagine that chew toys don't last too long with dozens of energetic critters sharing them!)

Lots of kids participated in the annual March for the Animals fundraiser, marching with their own pets and raising money from family, friends and neighbors. Sometimes I saw Scout troops weeding the grounds, planting flowers and otherwise helping make the shelter a nicer place for the staff, volunteers and animals.

Digital Deed: **Your kids can become promoters of your local rescue organization. They can link to the group's Facebook page, Twitter or other social media platforms so their contacts see pictures and descriptions of pets available for adoption and the dates and locations of adoption events. Some shelters might even welcome help with photography and posting of adoptable pets on their social media sites.**

PROFILE IN GENEROSITY:

Becoming a Foster Family

Lois Baron's two kids had been lobbying for a dog for a long time, so she and her husband, Jeff, finally acquiesced. At an adoption event near their Arlington, VA, home, they fell for a medium-size black mutt who had been a stray. Baron's daughter Nora, then age 9, learned that the rescue organization sponsoring the event didn't have its own shelter, but brought abandoned animals from overcrowded shelters in rural areas of the state to be adopted in the more populous area of Northern Virginia. All of the group's animals were in foster homes until permanent adoptions could be arranged. And there were never enough foster families. "After she found out that animals were dying in the shelters, Nora begged to save the animals," Baron said.

To sign on as a foster family, they had to go through a process similar to adoption—fill out paperwork and have a home visit. They also had to commit to taking their foster pet to adoption events twice a month. After they were accepted into the program, the family was assigned a small dog to care for. They named him Foster. It helped that the Baron family's own dog is mellow and didn't mind hosting a canine visitor.

One concern parents have is the attachment kids can form to the foster pets. Baron had to deal with that, especially when the family started fostering. "I helped them remember that we were getting the pet ready for its permanent family," she said. Sometimes the adopting families send pictures so Baron's kids can see their former fosters happily settled in their new homes.

Though it was Nora's idea, the whole family participates in animal care and attends adoption events. The rescue organization covers the cost of vet care and food. The benefits, aside from the fun they've had with the animals, are the lessons they've learned. "Fostering made my kids aware of how different animals are and how you can't judge them just by the way they look," Baron said. It also helped her kids realize that "not everyone has a home or enough food." They've had fosters that came from families with foreclosed homes, and they had one originally owned by a family displaced in Hurricane Katrina.

Helping Raise Service Dogs

If your children have seen someone with a disability who has an assistance dog, they might be interested to know that volunteers made that possible. Service dog organizations need puppy raisers to care for specially bred dogs until they are old enough for service training. The puppy raiser helps socialize the dog, gets it used to other people and being in public places, sometimes takes it to obedience classes, and generally provides love and care until the puppy matures. Volunteer rules vary. For example, some require puppy raisers to be at least 18 but allow younger volunteers if a parent or legal guardian is a co-applicant. To find a program near you, do an Internet search for "service dogs."

More Innovative Animal Ideas

- The oxygen masks fire fighters use to revive fire victims are the right size for people but not for pets. Kids and adults around the country are rectifying that by holding fundraisers to equip their local fire departments. Already, countless pets have been saved and families who have lost their homes have been spared losing beloved pets, too. Children are also helping raise funds to buy bullet-proof vests for their local police Canine Corps. If your kids are interested in such a project, contact your local fire or police department to see what they need.

- The Berks County, PA, Animal Rescue League has a program called Book Buddies for children in grades 1-8. It started with a staff member who had a 10-year-old struggling with reading in school. She brought him to the shelter to read to the cats in the adoption room, and he not only loved it, but has greatly improved his reading skills. The staff at this and other shelters with similar programs says animals find comfort in the rhythmic sound of a young person's voice. Now the shelter has a steady stream of Book Buddies.

TIP: *Go to berksarl.org for "awwww"-inspiring photos of kids reading to cats. If you feel inspired, contact a local shelter near you and offer to set up a similar program.*

- If you have a well-behaved pet that enjoys being around people, your family might be welcomed at a nursing home or hospice. Patients who may miss their own pets, or who just love to pet a furry friend, would be very grateful.

- Therapeutic riding programs are a popular volunteer project for kids who love horses. These programs serve children and adults who are physically or mentally challenged. Volunteers lead the horses. I know of a Mother-Daughter Philanthropy Club started by some families in California that made this a year-long activity.

TIP: *To find a program in your area, go to the Professional Association of Therapeutic Horsemanship International website (pathintl.org) for a locator of their member centers.*

Food, Glorious Food

Feeding the hungry is one of the fundamental tenets of philanthropy. All children can relate, even when they come from families with well stocked refrigerators. They know how it feels to be ravenous when they come home from school or after playing sports. In countless story books, kids who misbehave are punished by being sent to bed without supper. Children can imagine, at least a little, what it would be like not to have enough to eat. Unfortunately for some children, going to bed without dinner is all too real.

Although hunger is a major problem—in our own country and abroad—it's one that is solvable *if we have the collective will.* My husband Tom helped former Congressman Tony Hall write a book called *Changing the Face of Hunger* (W Publishing Group, 2006). A former U.S. Ambassador to the U.N. Agencies for Food and Agriculture, Hall is a longtime crusader for people in need. He wrote about meeting Mother Teresa in Calcutta and asking her "how we could hope to solve the problems of the hungry, the sick, the poor and the oppressed since there is such an overwhelming number of them." She replied: "You do what is in front of you." Hall said that "the lesson I took from her answer is this: If all of us did what was in front of us, think how many problems we would solve."

Digital Deed: Feeding America (feedingamerica.org), a nationwide network of food banks, engages virtual volunteers through its Spread the Word Campaign. Through social media, kids and families can share information and videos about how to end hunger. That's also where you can search for a food bank in your area.

Bill Shore, founder of Share Our Strength, decided to focus on hungry children. The goal of SOS is to end childhood hunger in America by ensuring children get healthy food every day—one in five does not. Through its No Kid Hungry campaign, SOS enlists countless volunteers in a variety of projects including one familiar to many families, originally the Great American Bake Sale, which SOS renamed Bake Sale No Kid Hungry. This is an easy way to engage kids. They'll hone their baking skills while also learning about promotion and sales. They can even earn community service hours for school requirements, all while raising money to help prevent other kids from going hungry.

The No Kid Hungry website (nokidhungry.org) is also a great place for families to learn more about the problem of hunger. In the parents' resource section, there are some helpful videos including one that explains why, in one of the most prosperous nations in the world, kids go hungry.

Digital Deed: Take pictures of your projects and post them on social media to inspire others to start their own generosity projects. (Note: It's important to protect other people's privacy. If you are working with a nonprofit that serves others, make sure photos are okay.)

Generous Gardens

What child doesn't love watching something grow? We all remember elementary school lessons involving seeds grown in paper cups of dirt—very exciting unless you were the kid with the brown thumb whose marigold never quite flowered. About two decades ago, Alice Waters, owner of the renowned Berkeley restaurant Chez Panisse, kicked gardening up a notch. She started her first Edible School Yard at a nearby elementary school to teach children about growing organic food and cooking and eating fresh food. Academic lessons are incorporated, too, and the model has inspired food education efforts at schools all over the country and abroad.

Waters helped inspire First Lady Michelle Obama, who created a garden on the White House grounds in 2009 to help promote healthy eating. The many elementary school classes from the Washington, DC area who help tend the garden also get an important lesson in philanthropy. One third of the garden's bounty is donated to Washington area food banks. The children learn that gardening is one way they can take action against hunger. This is all too real for many Washington children whose families have to rely on food banks to stretch their meals each month.

Kids who don't live in Washington can get in on the act. The Garden Writers Association's Plant a Row for the Hungry encourages families with gardens to plant an extra row and donate that produce to a nearby food bank or soup kitchen. The association estimates that, since the program began in 1995, more than 18 million pounds of produce providing over 72 million meals have been donated by American gardeners, about a million pounds a year. Families that don't have a garden might join forces with a neighbor who does, providing sweat equity in exchange for a portion of the crop.

TIP: *To find places to donate food, go to AmpleHarvest.org and plug in your zip code to locate soup kitchens and food pantries closest to you. The FAQ section for gardeners has helpful advice.*

PROFILE IN GENEROSITY:

The Tale of the 40 Pound Cabbage

I was watching a home and garden television show when the host introduced her guest—a young girl named Katie Stagliano who had grown a 40 pound cabbage that fed 275 people! This kid with the green thumb on steroids got my attention.

In 2008, when she was 8 and in third grade, Katie, from Summerville, SC, came home with a school assignment to plant a cabbage seed. With careful watering and fertilizing, it grew massive. Then the question was what to do with it. Katie wrote in her blog that at dinner one night, her father said the family should be grateful that they always had healthy meals when some families "were not able to put food on their tables, therefore were going to bed hungry. It was at that moment that I decided to donate the cabbage I had been growing to a soup kitchen." Her mother checked around and found one that would gladly accept the unusual donation and incorporate it into a meal. "When I walked in, I saw a huge line of people waiting for what might be the only meal they would have that day. The people who worked there and who were eating there were so friendly and nice. As I served my cabbage to the guests and they thanked me for helping to feed them, I knew I could and I should do more to help."

What followed was proof of the impact a child can have, especially with supportive family and friends. Her dream "was to end hunger one vegetable garden at a time." She talked her school into planting a large garden for all the students, grades K through 12, to tend, and the whole crop was donated to feeding programs. Later, a farmer offered more space, and a greenhouse was built. Nurseries and garden stores donated plants, tools and supplies. Katie didn't want to just grow healthy food, she wanted to cook and serve it, too. Every month, a swarm of Katie's friends, their parents and other helpful adults serve a meal in space provided by a local church. More than 100 people a month are served at the free dinners.

Not content to work only in Summerville, she started a nonprofit called Katie's Krops—she's the chief gardening officer—to inspire kids around the country to start gardens to feed the hungry. In 2014, there were 60 gardens organized by kids across the country. In recognition of her work, the Clinton Global Initiative honored Katie in 2012, with one of its annual Global Citizen Awards presented in New York City. Actor Matt Damon, who gave her the award, noted that at age 14, Katie was the youngest recipient ever, and that she was being honored "for proving that one person can grow an entire movement in their own back yard."

TIP: *Katie's Krops provides grants to kids 9 to 16 to launch their own gardens to feed people in need. Winners receive a gift card for a nearby garden center, financial support from Katie's Krops and a digital camera to record their garden's progress. All types of gardens are eligible: container gardens in cities, neighborhood gardens, school yard gardens, etc. The website (katieskrops.org) also has garden tips, recipes and a picture of Katie holding the 40 pound cabbage that started it all.*

If You Can't Grow Your Own, Try Gleaning

Gleaning—collecting excess food—goes back to Biblical times. Our neighbors Greg and Maureen Gannon made gleaning part of their family's summer and fall outings, taking their four young daughters to glean with other families from their church. They'd travel to a farm to harvest vegetables or fruits that didn't meet the appearance standards of supermarket shoppers but were still perfectly edible. The bounty went to a food bank. They loved these outings. Gleaning was great exercise, involved all ages, even toddlers, and included picnicking and fun with friends. All that and feeding the hungry, too? A perfect project.

Except that gleaning from farmers' fields is more for families living close to rural areas. The huge growth in farmers markets, especially in cities, is giving every family more opportunities to be gleaners. Many sellers donate products that are left at the end of the day. Volunteers are needed to sort, pack and deliver the goods to food pantries and soup kitchens. Community gardens are another place where families can organize gleaning. Restaurants and caterers have gotten into the act, too, sometimes using volunteers—usually organized in cooperation with nearby food banks—to pick up excess food.

Legislation passed by Congress in 1996—the Emerson Good Samaritan Food Donation Act—has helped to further gleaning efforts. Donors of excess food are protected from criminal and civil liability as long as they aren't grossly negligent.

TIP: *The U.S. Department of Agriculture website, usda.gov, has a helpful toolkit called "Let's Glean!" which is full of ideas and resources for individuals and families.*

From Julie

I learned from a friend who attended Marquette University about an organization she volunteered with that repurposed leftover cafeteria food into healthy meals for the homeless. Intrigued, I decided to learn more about the Campus Kitchens Project (campuskitchens.org). I discovered it was a spinoff of DC Central Kitchen in Washington. I reached out to their national office to learn how I might be able to get a CKP set up at my own college. They gave me everything I needed to approach the college administration and obtain all the necessary approvals. With a committed group of other students on board, who had heard about the fledgling CKP through other campus anti-hunger groups, the pieces started falling into place my senior year. I graduated before the first CKP meal was served. But the team was ready to get cooking that fall. Today, the College of William & Mary CKP has nearly 100 student volunteers who cook 175 meals in a local church basement every week. They deliver the meals—10,000 each year!—to local families in need. Ten years ago, there weren't very many schools that had CKP chapters. But today, there are 39 high schools and colleges around the country cooking up healthy meals out of reclaimed food. Talk about impact!

Food Drives: What to Do...and Not Do

A time-honored way kids and families have helped fight hunger is by collecting canned goods for food pantries. There's some debate about food drives. Some say it's better to just donate money so the pantry can buy exactly what it needs, especially since many of them purchase in bulk and their buying power means they can obtain more food for the money than an individual can. But some food programs, especially smaller ones, rely heavily on donations from such drives, and most food pantries welcome both kinds of donations. And let's face it, kids find it more tangible—and fun—to collect a mound of cans than to write a check. Even kids whose families don't have a lot of money can participate if the donation is a few cans of food.

The one time that canned food drives are definitely discouraged is during disasters. Relief agencies working in an area that has been devastated by a hurricane or flood would much rather have money to buy exactly what the affected people need. Food pantry facilities may have been destroyed, making it impossible to deal with truckloads of cans donated by people far away. A classic example was during the aftermath of the 2010 earthquake in Haiti. Some well-intentioned people donated baby formula. The hitch was it had to be mixed with clean water, and the affected areas had none. In cases of disaster, it's best to donate to groups on the ground that know what is most needed.

TIP: *DoSomething.org has a list of ideas for how teens can hold successful food drives. Examples: Host a movie night and charge a can of food for admission; set up a competition among classrooms to bring in the most; hold a raffle where donated cans earn chances for the prize.*

Things to Keep in Mind for Your Child's Canned Food Drive:

- Check with the food pantry before you start so you know what the organization does and doesn't need. When promoting your drive, provide a list of preferred items. This minimizes the chance of getting unusual items that recipients can't easily incorporate in meals.

- If possible, arrange a tour of the food bank with your kids before the drive so they can learn about hunger in their community and how the food pantry works.

- Many food pantries have resources on their websites for holding a successful food drive, such as sample promotional materials.

- Many drives are run during Thanksgiving and the December holidays so it might be more helpful to conduct a drive in the spring or summer.

- Food pantries don't need just food. They also need onsite volunteers to sort and pack food or perform other tasks. Check to see if there is one in your community that will allow families with younger children or teens on their own to volunteer.

PROFILE IN GENEROSITY:

A Family Affair

Each year, on a day in early December, our neighborhood finds that grocery bags with fliers attached have been dropped at our doorsteps. (A local supermarket provides the bags in exchange for the free advertising.) We're asked to put canned goods and other nonperishable food items in the bag and place it by the door on a designated Saturday when the bags are magically whisked away. What we don't usually see are the countless moms and dads driving around early in the morning with their kids hopping out of vehicles and fanning out on each block to drop and later retrieve the bags at all those doorsteps.

This holiday tradition started in the 1980s when our wonderful neighbor Greg Gannon, a parishioner at a nearby Catholic church, started the food drive with the help of his wife Maureen, their four daughters, and a small group of family and friends (yes, the same family mentioned earlier in the section on gleaning). Gradually, more families started volunteering as a way to teach their kids about giving. For many, it has become an annual ritual—the kick-off to their holidays.

Greg died in 2006 of brain cancer at the age of 55. His legacy, now called the Greg Gannon Food Drive, is run by his brother Rick, and has grown to 600 volunteers who collect a whopping 85,000 cans annually to distribute to numerous food banks and soup kitchens in the Washington, DC area.

Digital Deed: **Kids can run a "Virtual Food Drive" by using social media to encourage donations of money to a designated organization rather than actual canned goods. The Maryland Food Bank, for example, has an online supermarket where donors can "shop" for needed items, e.g., a case of 24 cans of applesauce for about $15, for example. Since the food bank buys from a consortium, it can purchase four times as much for the same amount of money as an individual can in a grocery store. The food bank can also use the donations to buy food other than canned, such as fresh produce.**

Pantries for Pets

People aren't the only ones needing food. Economic hard times hit families with pets, too. A donation of kibble can mean a family can keep a beloved cat or dog until they get back on their feet financially. Some food pantries for people have started stocking pet food. Now there are even food pantries specifically for pets.

Environmental Issues

Many children are drawn to the idea of being good stewards of the earth. A variety of projects fall under this heading, from planting trees to recycling cans. Here are some ideas:

- Weed flower beds and plant flowers at a local park or school.

- Pick up trash—in parks, in school yards or along stream beds.

- Give your child a role in separating your recyclables from your household trash.

- Show your electric bill to your kids and put them in charge of reducing it, by turning off lights when not in use, for example. Offer to give them the savings on a subsequent electric bill to donate to their favorite charity.

PROFILE IN GENEROSITY:

Souper Bowl of Caring

It started with a simple prayer: "Lord, even as we enjoy the Super Bowl football game, help us be mindful of those who are without a bowl of soup to eat." It was delivered by Brad Smith, then a seminary intern serving at a Presbyterian church in Columbia, SC, and it spawned a youth movement. Teams of kids turn party-filled Super Bowl weekends into a higher purpose by collecting money and canned goods to feed the hungry. Started in 1990, the movement now has 7,000 groups who collected $8 million in cash and food in 2013. Everything the youth collect goes directly to a local charity they choose.

When the youth group at our church held big soup pots outside the doors of the sanctuary one Super Bowl Sunday at the end of the worship service, congregants filled them with cash. Many knew they were going home to lavish party spreads and were reminded that some people wouldn't have a decent meal that day. (Go to souperbowl.org to learn more.)

- Encourage your kids to regularly go through their gently used toys and clothes for things they no longer want but that could be donated to a charity that would put them to good use.

- Talk about your carbon footprint. For example, your family can help save the earth's energy resources—and reduce carbon emissions—by walking sometimes instead of using gas in the family car or by turning down the thermostat in winter and piling on an extra blanket.

Digital Deed: **You can find a carbon calculator at MeetTheGreens.pbskids.org. This fun site, for kids and tweens, has short videos about The Green Family, plus games, ideas and a downloadable activity guide. Public television station WBGH in Boston created the site to encourage kids to explore green living.**

Read Stories about the Environment

You can start some great conversations by reading books with your kids. Dr. Seuss's *The Lorax* is a classic example (and spawned a popular movie). One of Julie's and my all-time favorite children's books is *Miss Rumphius* by Barbara Cooney. It's a beautifully illustrated story that answers the question "Why are we here?" Miss Rumphius returns from her worldwide travels to her tiny seaside village where she scatters lupine seeds on her walks. The next spring, the whole area blooms with a profusion of colorful flowers. After you read this book, consider giving your children packets of lupine or other wild flowers to plant.

The Great Outdoors

Some outdoor projects are not about planting but about ripping out plants. We live close to Rock Creek Park, one of the largest urban parks in the country. Invasive species—non-native plants that harm native habitats—have become a real problem, so volunteers young and old regularly organize to pull the weeds. One teenager who lives nearby took this on as his Eagle Scout project and arranged crews on two or three weekends through our neighborhood listserv. Many communities have projects like this. Contact your local parks department to find one. Another popular project in our part of the country is collecting tree seeds. In September and October, kids and adults gather acorns, walnuts and other seeds and turn them in at drop off locations in Maryland, Pennsylvania, Virginia and West Virginia. The seeds of native hardwood trees are then used to grow seedlings for planting along the Potomac River watershed to stem erosion in sensitive streamside forests. Seeds can be collected in your backyard—if you have the right kind of trees—or from your neighborhood or in public collection areas designated by the conservation organization. See growingnative.org, then explore whether a local conservation group in your area has a similar program.

Finding Group Projects

Scout troops, religious congregations, schools, after-school programs and summer camps are places where kids may learn about environmental issues and work together to become better stewards of the earth. Pre-teens and teens often are drawn to environment clubs at school. If they want to explore starting clubs, here are a few places to check out:

Roots and Shoots (rootsandshoots.org) was founded by famed primatologist and environmentalist Jane Goodall to provide a framework for groups that want to engage children and youth around environmental issues. The model is flexible and allows the young people to design, lead and implement their own projects customized to the group's interests. There are clubs in 100 countries. By joining the network, you get access to project guides and many other resources for starting a club.

GenerationOn, the youth and family division of Points of Light, is a global youth service movement for kids and teens. The site has ideas for projects, including a section on helping the environment, plus resources for parents and teachers (generationon.org). DoSomething.org usually has at least one environmentally-related campaign going at any given time, which youth can do individually or together.

TIP: *The U.S. Environmental Protection Agency has a site for kids in grades K-12 with ideas for service projects, science fair projects and homework resources on the environment, plus games, quizzes and information on the President's Environmental Youth Awards. It's also a good site for parents and teachers. Go to epa.gov/students.*

Giving of Themselves—Literally

Blood Donations

A blood donation is more precious than gold for the person whose life hangs in the balance. A donor has to be at least 17 years old in most states, but some allow teens as young as 16 to donate with parental approval. The Red Cross website has tips and videos to acquaint teens with the process and the eligibility requirements such as minimum heights and weights for boys and girls. There's also a section for student athletes who are advised, for example, not to give blood on the same day as a game or strenuous practice since the body needs time to replenish lost fluid, usually no more than 24 hours and less if you drink extra liquids.

The site also has a guide for parents about young people giving blood, and a place to insert your zip code to download the parental permission form required by your state.

TIP: *Maybe your student could recruit others to go with her to give blood. Friends, members of a school club or a sports team could make it a group activity. If your teenager doesn't qualify as a donor, he can still organize a blood drive and promote it through social media.*

From Julie

When I waited to give blood for the first time in my high school's gym, I was pretty nervous. (It didn't help that I had to watch a member of the baseball team—clearly bigger and stronger than me—nearly pass out before finishing his donation.) But my dad had been a long-time donor, and had explained to me, from the time I was a little kid, about why he donated. He came to my school that day to give blood next to me, which made the experience less frightening. I braved the scary needle, and though I did get lightheaded (they were running a bit behind schedule so I'd missed lunch), it wasn't bad at all. I've continued to donate when I can (it doesn't take much time, and you can only do it every eight weeks), and have given over a gallon of blood since that first donation in high school. And I never turn down the free cookies and orange juice!

Organ and Tissue Donations

Does your driver's license say you are an organ donor? What about your son's or daughter's? If so, you are part of a group of more than 100 million people in the U.S. who have registered, according to the U.S. Department of Health and Human Services. Still, as medical advances make more life-saving transplants possible, HHS says the gap continues to widen between the number of donors and the number of people on the waiting lists. People of all ages and backgrounds can be organ and tissue donors. Young people can also register in advance to express their wishes about organ donation. Where we live, in the District of Columbia, for example, a child can join the donation registry at age 13. But until she turns 18, the parents make the final decision about organ or tissue donation if the time comes.

There is a lot that youth can do to recruit more donors. The director of an organ donor registry in a southern state told me that several years ago he enlisted members of a local 4-H Club to help him distribute organ donor cards. But the kids didn't stop there. They made posters, created public service announcements and organized drives, all before social media even existed. The director said he could not have increased the organization's donor numbers without the help of those creative, energetic club members.

Young people are also involved in Be the Match, an effort by the National Marrow Donor Program to identify potential matches for blood cancer patients. Anyone between 18 and 60 can register—it just requires filling out a questionnaire, then taking a swab from inside your cheek (from a kit that is mailed to you). Teens too young to qualify can still promote the cause through social media.

From Julie

When I got to the College of William and Mary, there were tons of fliers and events for the school's bone marrow drive—the largest college registry drive in the country. I thought about joining the registry, but I had to think through whether I'd really be able to go through with it if I ever got a call that I'd been matched. Though I knew the likelihood of ever being someone's match was slim, donating bone marrow is an invasive medical procedure with the potential for some real discomfort. But then I thought about Jordan, Eve and Julia, three little kids I used to babysit in high school who had lost their dad to a rare bone marrow cancer, the same one my grandmother died of. I knew that if a transplant could give someone like him a little more time with their family, I'd want to do it.

TIP: *The U.S. Department of Health and Human Services website (hhs.gov) has a section on how college students can organize organ donor registration drives on their campuses. A similar guide for the Be the Match marrow donor drive can be found at marrow.org.*

Helping the Elderly

Even if kids don't live close to their grandparents, they may know senior citizens in their neighborhood. Some of those neighbors need more help as they age. This is an opportunity to "adopt a grandparent." People who don't get out much would probably enjoy a friendly visit, a gift of home-baked cookies with a home-made card, or offers to take the senior's dog for a walk, run some errands, rake leaves or shovel snow off sidewalks. Seniors who are visually impaired may enjoy having young people read to them.

TIP: *A fast-growing number of "senior villages" are being established in neighborhoods across the country. These membership organizations help older residents continue living in their homes by arranging services such as transportation, home maintenance and social activities. Each village sets its own policy about volunteers, but there are often opportunities for families and teens. Sometimes school groups organize spring and fall garden cleanups for senior village members, for example, to earn community service credit. Contact your local office of aging or the Village to Village Network (vtvnetwork.org) to find a village near you.*

Going Global

When children woke up on Oct. 11, 2013, some of them anxiously asked their parents who had won the Nobel Peace Prize. They had hoped that a 16-year-old nominee would take the award, the youngest person ever nominated. Malala Yousafzai didn't win that year, but she already had earned rock star status with kids—and adults—around the world. Her biography, *I Am Malala*, was released days before, and she had been interviewed by countless news media about having taken a stand for girls' education and been shot by the Taliban for her actions. (Her fans were rewarded the following year when Malala was one of two people awarded the peace prize.)

Her activism started early. She was only 11 when she began her crusade, writing a blog under a pseudonym for the BBC about life under the Taliban, which controlled the valley in Northwest Pakistan where she lived. A year later she was filmed for a *New York Times* documentary, and began giving broadcast interviews. The Taliban decided to silence her. On Oct. 9, 2012, an assassin boarded her school bus, called her name, and shot her in the head and neck. Miraculously, she survived after three months of treatment and several surgeries in a hospital in England, where she was taken a few days after the attack.

Her story inspired others. In April, 2013, her face graced the cover of *Time*, which named her one of the 100 most influential people in the world. On July 12, 2013, Malala's 16th birthday, she spoke at the United Nations, her first speech since the attack, to call for worldwide access to education.

"It feels like this life is not my life. It's a second life," she once said. "People have prayed to God to spare me and I was spared for a reason— to use my life for helping people."

 **Malala Yousafzai's nonprofit, the Malala Fund (malalafund.org), stresses that "education empowers girls to raise their voices, to unlock their potential, and to demand change." The fund works with local partners around the world on girl-centric approaches to education. Kids can sign up for updates on the fund's Facebook page, and can also help spread the word.**

Malala's powerful story is just one example of how today's youth don't just consider the needs of their local communities. Their perspective is global. They know more about the world than any previous generation. Some of the reasons include: coverage on the Internet and news media, the increase of diversity in the communities they grow up in, lessons in school and more international travel by young people.

International adoptions have had an influence, too. Kids who are adopted from other countries are often taught about their native land, and they may want to help the orphanages where they came from or other causes in their country of origin. Beth Kanter, a blogger and expert on nonprofits' use of social media, and the co-author of *The Networked Nonprofit*, has involved her two adopted children in giving projects all their lives. But one especially close to her heart and theirs is the Sharing Foundation. In 2012, she took her then-preteen son and daughter to Cambodia where she introduced them to their birth country, and showed them the work of the Sharing Foundation, which helps orphaned and seriously disadvantaged Cambodian children.

One drawback to international giving for most kids is that it's harder to find projects they can get involved in directly instead of just sending money. If your family is interested in international work, one way to find opportunities is through organizations you are already connected with, such as your school, civic group or religious congregation. Our church, for example, has long supported a school, orphanage and health clinic in a village in Kenya. Periodically, a few church members, including a doctor, go to the village to see the progress and lend a hand. And they take a big load of colorful Crocs for the village children. These indestructible rubber shoes, so popular with U.S. kids, are donated by our church's children when they outgrow them. The shoes are very popular with the village children, too.

Girl Up

The United Nations Foundation has created a way for girls (and boys) to get involved in the movement to help adolescent girls in other countries go to school, get access to health care and stay safe from violence. The UNF's Girl Up clubs exist in every state and in 33 countries. Jules Spector, a 14-year-old from Brooklyn, started a Girl Up club in her middle school. But she'd been thinking about the plight of girls abroad long before that.

When she was 9, the avid reader found a book on her mother's desk called *Half the Sky* by journalists Nicholas Kristof and Cheryl WuDunn, about the status of girls and women in developing countries. She was shocked by what she read. "I thought all girls went to school," she recalled, "and I didn't know the problems they faced. I was in a protective bubble, and it broke my heart to read these stories. I thought about it for a long time, but I didn't know how to help." In 2012, she discovered Girl Up clubs and worked with two teachers to start one. To raise funds to support U.N. Foundation efforts, her club sells soda at sports events, and, to raise awareness, puts up posters and make presentations to other students.

"Today's teens have global reach," Jules said. "We have lifestyles geared around social media. We can advocate for change by tweeting, posting on Facebook and getting people to be part of an organization you believe strongly in." She's also used Instagram to share pictures of club events. She believes in the impact children can have. "It's a proven fact that lifting up girls and women improves whole communities. If you help girls get an education, get them out of child marriages and brothels, if you invest in girls, that's key to reducing poverty. Everything will change."

Jules is particularly concerned about forced child marriages. "I get really angry when a 7-year-old is engaged to a 40-year-old, and I use my anger to tell people about these issues."

Leadership training is also part of the Girl Up model. Jules is a teen advisor for Girl Up, and got to meet Malala Yousafzai. "It was an amazing experience," Jules said. "The Taliban thought they could silence her, but she just became louder."

TIP: *Boys can join Girl Up clubs, too, or they can support the cause by signing a pledge or raising money. Also, you don't have to start a Girl Up club to get involved. Go to the website, girlup.org, and click on Take Action.*

The book *Half the Sky* has spawned a movement that includes a four-hour TV series on PBS, websites, games and blogs to raise awareness of the issues and to give people concrete steps they can take to empower women and girls.

 Want more ideas for projects? See Chapter 10 on holidays and family celebrations.

CHAPTER 6:

Money Know-How

I would rather have it said,
'He lived usefully,' than, 'He died rich.'

Benjamin Franklin (letter to his mother, 1750)

When Julie was young, she didn't understand why, when people needed money, they couldn't just go to the ATM. The concept of how those seemingly free-flowing bills got in there—and why they'd stop coming out—was hard to explain to a pre-schooler.

Any discussion of raising giving children needs to include something about financial literacy. If kids don't know how to manage money, they'll never have any to give away. And they could grow up to be adults burdened with debt without any savings to cope with unexpected circumstances. Habits around money, for better or worse, are largely formed when we are very young. Some children spend every cent they get, some squirrel away all their cash and some take the middle ground. It's not uncommon for two siblings to take completely opposite approaches.

One of the most important things you can do for your children—whether you are on the high or low end of the income scale—is to teach them at a young age to manage money.

In earlier chapters we covered sharing. Now let's talk about spending and saving.

Allowances Are a Powerful Tool

If we want children to learn how to manage money, they need some to practice with. If they are mature enough to understand that a tiny dime has more buying power than a nickel, they're ready for an allowance, usually around age 6. Having their own money, even a small amount, means they can make choices about whether a toy is worth the price or whether they'd rather buy something now or save up for something more expensive later.

One question I'm often asked is "How much should I give my child?" The answer depends on what your child's allowance will be expected to cover. Once your kids have their own money, they should be made responsible for some purchases you'd have covered in the past. For young children with a small allowance, maybe you'll no longer pay for small toys or for treats from the ice cream truck. When they ask for something, remind them they can pay for it themselves. I guarantee your kids will think harder about how much they really want the item if the price is coming out of their own pockets. They might still buy that treat but, with limited funds, they will learn from experience the value of delayed gratification.

Some families require their children to pay for gifts for others. Some parents also require a certain percentage be given to charity. Do what feels right for your family. If you don't mandate a portion for charity, you can still encourage charitable giving by offering to match your child's donations. Having twice as much to give to something he or she is passionate about creates an extra incentive.

For teens, an allowance may need to cover entertainment, such as movie tickets or eating out with friends. When Julie entered high school, she wanted more freedom to buy her own clothes. We settled on a clothing budget that was pretty lean. She quickly became a savvy bargain shopper who waited for sales and browsed thrift stores to make her budget stretch. She also earned extra money babysitting. She loved not having to ask us whenever she wanted a new outfit.

Some parents start with $1 a week for each year of the child's age. It makes sense that older siblings receive a higher amount than younger ones, and that they are responsible for covering more of their expenses. If you decide to require that the allowance be divided into thirds—for spending, sharing and saving, as some parents prefer—make it an amount that's easily divisible by three or it becomes an accounting nightmare.

TIP: *Give young children banks to keep their money in, but pick transparent ones so they can see their cash growing (or not, if they spend it immediately). Some parents like to use three jars—labeled saving, sharing and spending—to help kids keep their pots straight. As preparation for balancing a checkbook (or online bank account), some parents also give their children small notebooks where they can record their income and expenses.*

Let Them Learn the Hard Way

Unless your children want to use their money for something harmful or that violates your family's values, let them decide how to spend it. For example, you can nix a toy that isn't safe for kids their age, or draw the line at violent video games or clothes you deem inappropriate. Otherwise, if your child covets a toy advertised on TV, and you have doubts about how well it will hold up or think it's overpriced, it is better not to interfere. This is how children learn to be critical shoppers and to measure "sorta wants" vs. "gotta haves." If the toy falls apart in hours, that's an important lesson. You could casually introduce some conversation about how you assess your own purchases for quality and value. But go easy on the guidance at this stage.

The Lessons of Saving

One way kids learn about money is by watching their parents. When you take them shopping, talk about your purchases in the context of your family's limited household budget and the choices you have to make. An allowance will give them personal experience with this concept. But the lesson will be lost if you give them an allowance and still pay for whatever they want.

Julie was in elementary school when American Girl dolls became all the rage. Several of her friends had them. (One friend's grandmother had bought her three!) But Julie didn't play much with the dolls she already had, and I balked at the $85 price tag. I told her if she wanted it, she'd have to save her allowance. It took her more than a year, and I felt like the meanest mother in town, but there was never a prouder day than when that 9-year-old turned her savings into the coveted doll. And, as I predicted, Julie seldom played with it. But the doll is still one of her treasured possessions, carefully stored in pristine condition, to be passed down to another child someday. Don't think we never bought her presents or treats. I didn't want that meanest mother label to stick! But mostly, her buying power lay in savings from her allowance.

If your child is in a store and leaning toward an impulse purchase, suggest he go home and sleep on it, and offer to bring him back to the store the next day if he still wants the item. Chances are the impulse won't be so strong. A waiting period also gives him time to see how much the purchase will impact his piggy bank.

Older kids can find online resources that let them create budgets and keep track of their spending, saving and sharing.

Digital Deed: **Suggest your child do a little online research before making a big purchase. For example, he can look the item up on a site such as Amazon that posts customer comments. Older kids can tap their social media network to see whether their friends recommend the item.**

Teaching the Value of Investing

Some kids just stuff their savings in a jar. Others learn that putting their money where it earns interest will help their balance grow. Some banks have tapped into the child market with low- or no-fee accounts. Kids can check their balance and transfer money online with the help of a parent. But interest rates at banks are often too small to be very meaningful. My husband Tom decided to create his own bank for our daughter in her elementary school years. It was basically a computer file where he listed a "deposit" of each week's allowance and deducted any money she spent. At the end of the month he added 10 percent interest to whatever was in her account and provided her with a printout. Even though that compound interest was a huge amount compared to the paltry sums banks were offering, he wanted her to have a meaningful amount so she could really see her savings grow. She embraced the lesson almost too well. Eventually Tom had to slash her interest rate because "the bank" ended up owing her so much!

Interest also is a two-way street. There may be occasions when a child asks for an advance on his allowance to make a special purchase. If you decide to make him a loan, consider charging him interest. The cost of borrowing money is another important lesson for children to learn before adulthood.

Some parents take investment lessons further by buying their child a share of stock in a company that makes products she likes, so she can learn about the stock market. Teens occasionally participate in investment clubs in schools. But it's those early habits of saving their allowance, started when children are very young, that will be valuable at every stage in life.

 **Digital Deed:** The President's Advisory Council on Financial Capability, created in 2010 by President Obama, seeks to improve financial literacy among all citizens. One focus is children. The council sponsors a website, MoneyAsYouGrow.org, which has age-appropriate lessons for kids as young as age 3.

Tying Allowances to Chores Can Backfire

Some parents require kids to do chores to "earn" their allowances, but that can be a trap. Chores should be required of all children as part of their contribution to the family. If the punishment for not doing chores is missing their allowance, some kids will choose to forgo the money. Then you don't have the tool to teach your kids money management, and they aren't contributing any help to the family. Instead, if they don't do their chores, take away a privilege such as video games or other screen time.

If, on the other hand, your children want to supplement their allowances, you can pay them for taking on specific jobs that are above and beyond their regular chores. This is especially attractive to kids who aren't old enough to take jobs outside the home, such as babysitting or lawn mowing.

Credit Cards for Kids?

When Julie was in high school, we added her name as an authorized user to a credit card we seldom used. It became "hers," but the bills still came to us and she had to pay off the balance every month. That way, she didn't have to carry cash when she went shopping, and she also learned how to use a credit card before she headed to college. There were some months when she had a rude awakening about how much she had charged, but the card carried a low credit limit and we were there to monitor things.

These days, some banks offer credit and debit cards for teens and allow parents to impose controls and oversee the account. There is no magic age when a teen is ready—some 13-year-olds are, while some 17-year-olds aren't responsible enough to handle one. Regardless, keep having conversations about managing credit responsibly.

From Julie

I know from personal experience that once kids head off to college, they're going to be inundated with pitches from credit card companies. They set up tables in the student center and flood students' campus mailboxes with offers. It's better to take advantage of the window when your kids are home to teach them about credit cards, because once they turn 18, they can get one whether they are prepared or not, and quite a few rack up big debt as a result.

How Schools Can Help

It troubles me that kids can leave high school with a solid knowledge of calculus but not a clue about compound interest. Only a few states require personal finance education. Some offer a stand-alone course; others incorporate it in courses such as math. Yet the National Association of State Boards of Education (nasbe.org), recommends financial literacy education be a basic feature of K-12 education.

Some financial firms, including credit card companies, have teamed with other organizations to offer online courses and video games. Some also provide grants to schools that use these programs. Many firms support the Jump$tart Coalition (jumpstart.org), a nonprofit focusing on advancing financial literacy in pre-schoolers through college-age youth. The Jump$tart website contains a wealth of resources, including lists of which financial skills and knowledge students in each K-12 grade should have.

Still, schools can't substitute for the kind of day-to-day financial education parents can provide, beginning with the pre-school set.

TIP: *Junior Achievement (juniorachievement.org) volunteers guide hands-on programs that educate K-12 students in nearly 200,000 classrooms about workforce readiness, entrepreneurship and financial literacy. Check out the website for free materials for parents of young kids through teenagers, and find out if your school has a Junior Achievement program.*

PROFILE IN GENEROSITY:

Views of the Mega-Wealthy

Two of the richest men in the world have made clear that they do not want their children to be spoiled by inherited wealth. Warren Buffett told Fortune *magazine in 1986 that he was leaving the bulk of his fortune to charity, because one should leave "enough money to your kids so they can do anything, but not enough so they can do nothing."*

In a 2011 interview with the British Daily Mail *newspaper, Bill Gates echoed a similar theme in discussing what his kids will inherit:*

"It will be a minuscule portion of my wealth. It will mean they have to find their own way. They will be given an unbelievable education and that will all be paid for. And certainly anything related to health issues we will take care of. But in terms of their income, they will have to pick a job they like and go to work. They are normal kids now. They do chores, they get pocket money."

CHAPTER 7:

Student Life

Do your little bit of good where you are.
It's those little bits of good put together that
overwhelm the world...

Archbishop Desmond Tutu

As a generosity coach, you aren't in this alone. More schools and colleges are making service a focus—part of their role as educators of well-rounded citizens. Let's start with K-12 schools. (Later in this chapter we'll cover what's happening on college campuses.)

A growing number of schools are offering community service opportunities and/or service learning. What's the difference? **Community service** generally refers to volunteering done outside of classes. **Service learning** incorporates a volunteer component into the curriculum. Both provide children the opportunity to learn about and engage in giving, which is especially valuable for those who haven't been exposed to volunteering at home. Student bodies are diverse in their experiences and attitudes. For some kids, the phrase "community service" is associated with punishment for committing a crime. Others may have been on the receiving end of charity and now welcome the opportunity to give back. Helping others through a school service project can make a positive difference to a child's sense of self-worth.

Community Service

Community service programs are becoming common in middle and high schools. In some school districts, service is mandatory. Students are required to volunteer a certain number of hours in order to graduate. Mandating service has been controversial. Some educators say that it can compete with academics and puts a burden on staff to track the students' hours. Some question whether kids get much out of the experience when it's not voluntary. And some nonprofits find it annoying to get calls every spring from seniors who want to volunteer for a few hours because they're a little short of their graduation requirement.

Advocates of the requirement contend that it produces some students' only volunteering experience. Required programs that are well executed can excite and engage students. The places where mandatory requirements have been shown to work effectively are in those school districts that obtain input from teachers, administrators, students, parents and the broader community throughout the planning and implementation phases.

Whether a program is mandatory or not, success depends on students having a leadership role. Peer influence is a powerful motivator. A culture of service can thrive in a school when volunteering is made a priority and it becomes a cool thing to do. Schools with voluntary programs still have the option of keeping track of hours and providing recognition for students who participate.

TIP: *Schools that engage their students in community service often welcome support from parents, especially in the lower grades. Schools may want help identifying appropriate volunteer projects in the community, or just need adults to chaperone or drive kids to activities. Some parent-teacher groups organize family service nights where students and their parents visit booths that offer simple projects, such as making sandwiches for a homeless shelter or writing cards for service men and women overseas. Help your child's school start a service program, and consider it your own volunteer project!*

PROFILE IN GENEROSITY:

Project Outreach

Norwich Free Academy, a 158- year-old high school in Norwich, CT, has a long history of service. A hybrid of sorts, Norwich is a blend of public and independent school that requires all student organizations and athletic teams to participate in at least one service project a year. But the real center of action is Project Outreach, a student volunteer and advocacy organization that could be a model for other schools.

Approximately 500 student volunteers serve at least one hour a week—most do more—during their study hall on campus and in nearly 50 organizations in the community. The school converted a classroom into a Project Outreach lounge, where students from every grade and from a variety of economic, linguistic and ethnic backgrounds work together. Project Outreach wasn't required, "but it was the cool thing to do," recalled one alumna. "It is a safe haven where all students can fit in."

Three Buckets

Youth philanthropy experts refer to "three buckets" in describing the levels of involvement in community service. If the cause is hunger, for example, the first bucket is bringing canned goods for a food drive. The second is taking a leadership role in organizing the food drive. The third bucket is thought leadership, where students identify and address the root causes of why people are hungry. The majority of kids in community service programs are in the first bucket, but to make real change, all three types of involvement are needed.

Psychologist Marilyn Price-Mitchell, Ph.D., writing in generationOn's "Ready-Set-Go" guide to youth volunteering, labels these buckets as Responsible Citizens, Leaders and Innovators. She writes that, ideally, young people move beyond the simple action of volunteering to become civically engaged. "Research shows that adolescents thrive when they are at the center of civic action, learning how to be leaders and innovators...To become civically engaged, adolescents require a different kind of adult scaffolding than children do. Adults should share power and decision-making with young people, allow them to learn from mistakes and reinforce their belief in themselves."

Service Learning

Service learning is less common in schools because it's more challenging than community service. It takes more teacher time and training. It can be difficult to arrange service time that fits into the school schedule. But there is a growing movement to incorporate service into the curriculum. Here are a couple of examples from Julie's high school:

A Spanish teacher created a partnership with a nearby Latino outreach center. Our students tutored theirs in English and they helped ours with Spanish. Our students helped produce the organization's bilingual newsletter for donors and shot a video of the center's programs, all the while brushing up their language skills in the real world rather than from textbooks.

Another teacher tried a more international approach. She helped her middle schoolers learn about the problem of land mines left over from armed conflicts and still lethal to children and adults many years later. Every time I drove the carpool, I heard about a problem I'd been only vaguely aware of, and I learned about advocacy efforts to get countries to sign on to an international treaty. The students turned their concern into action as they raised money to pay for a bomb-sniffing dog used by an international group working to detect and safely destroy the mines.

Service learning experts say key components of a good program are:

- Students have meaningful leadership roles.

- Learning and development goals tie the project to class content.

- Student projects meet a clear community need and are designed with community input.

- There are multiple sessions during which students investigate the problem, plan and execute a project to address it, then reflect on the project afterward.

TIP: *The National Youth Leadership Council maintains the National Service-Learning Clearinghouse, with thousands of free online resources for K-12 classes and colleges. The organization also developed learning standards for the field. Another resource is Youth Service America's Classrooms with a Cause, which helps K-12 teachers and students address community issues. Youth Service America also has created Semester of Service, with activities that are aligned with Common Core and other state standards and that last for a minimum of 12 to 14 weeks of continuous service-learning experiences.*

The Learning to Give Curriculum

One of the barriers to philanthropy education in schools is the contention that there is no room in an already packed curriculum to add one more topic. Some years ago, with foundation funding, the Learning to Give curriculum (learningtogive.org) was created. It's a compilation of more than 1,700 K-12 service learning lesson plans, all of which align with the Common Core State Standards, individual state standards and some international standards. The lessons, which are free and downloadable, are used in schools across the United States and in several other countries. By connecting academics with responsible citizenship, schools aim to develop the whole child. The lessons are infused into the existing curriculum. For example, when elementary school teachers cover the

Underground Railroad, they can frame it as an act of philanthropy: A widely dispersed group of caring people risked their lives to help others.

The need for teacher training is another barrier to service learning, but Learning to Give has that covered too, with 10 free, self-paced modules at its Fisher Online Institute.

TIP: *If you still read to your children, Learning to Give's section for parents has a list of excellent books with stories addressing giving and civic engagement. Each one comes with a literature guide that includes questions to ask your child before, during and after reading the book, and also has some fun and thought-provoking activities that relate to the story's theme. It's like having your very own adult/child book club!*

Alternative Spring Break

Who needs the beach? Some high schools and colleges now offer alternative spring breaks during which students spread out in communities across the country—and sometimes internationally—to volunteer in service projects ranging from repairing homes damaged by weather disasters to working with children in community centers to assisting on archeological digs. Typically, students pay a fee to cover food, lodging, project costs and local transportation. Students also are responsible for their travel to and from the city where they will work. Service-oriented summer camps are also gaining in popularity with teens.

Student United Way is a campus-based, student-led organization that works in partnership with local United Ways. Currently, there are Student United Ways on more than 60 campuses across the United States, including technical and trade schools, junior and community colleges, four-year colleges and universities and several high schools.

Some young people spend a gap year after high school performing community service. The American Gap Association (americangap.org) defines a gap year as "a structured period of time when students take a break from formal education to increase self-awareness, challenge comfort zones, and experiment with possible careers. Typically these are achieved by a combination of traveling, volunteering, interning or working."

PROFILE IN GENEROSITY:

A Buddy Bench

Too often when we learn of another school shooting, we find the perpetrator is a young person who was bullied or friendless. Slights on the school yard can eventually lead to a student becoming a bully himself or a loner with a lot of anger. Second-grader Christian Bucks of York, PA, probably wasn't thinking of all that when he got the idea for a "buddy bench" at his school. He just wanted a place for classmates to go when they felt lonely during recess. When other kids see someone on the bench, they can go talk to them or invite them to play.

According to the York Daily Record *(Dec. 2, 2013) Christian learned of the buddy bench concept when his dad was researching a possible move for work. The family investigated some international schools, including one in Germany, and Christian spotted the buddy bench in a school photo. The family took the idea to the principal who heartily approved and asked Christian to help with the bench design. Christian presented the idea at a school assembly to get other kids on board. As sometimes happens when a child comes up with a great—and compassionate—idea, the story in his hometown paper was picked up by other media and led to Christian appearing on the* Today *show and other national TV programs. Christian's instant celebrity interested other schools in creating a simple way to encourage peer support. And why not? Some of our best friendships are made on the playground.*

TIP: *The AGA's website has suggestions for how to vet gap year organizations. Also, United Way runs an alternative spring break program that matches students with many of the organizations it serves. Students can choose from national or local volunteer opportunities.*

From Julie

One day during college, I was flipping through a campus newsletter. I saw a small item about an alternative spring break trip to an orphanage in the Dominican Republic. A student who had participated in the program the previous year was organizing a group of volunteers, and in an unusually impulsive moment, I decided to sign up. I began fundraising to cover my costs for the week and also provide a nice donation to the nonprofit sponsoring the trip, Outreach360 (formerly Orphanage Outreach).

When the day of the trip arrived, I was anxious. I'd had to get some shots and medications (malaria pills! a polio booster shot!) because of the orphanage's location, and I didn't meet any of the other students going on the trip until we all arrived at the airport. Luckily, people bond with each other pretty quickly when jumping into a new experience together.

The week went by in a whirlwind. We met all of the children living at the orphanage, ranging in age from about 4 to 17, and learned their personal stories. We played games with them when they weren't in school, did maintenance work around the property, and spent a day volunteering at their school where we taught some English classes. I was lucky to be placed with some second graders, and we played a fun counting game to practice English numbers.

International volunteer trips have been in the news lately, and not usually for good reasons. There are legitimate questions about whether certain programs are well run, and how much of a positive impact a group of teens can have on a community in such a brief window of time. So do I feel like we made a difference in our week in Monte Cristi, DR?

We certainly did our best to be useful, and do whatever the on-the-ground staff asked of us. We kept the kids at the orphanage entertained, helped them practice their English, and showed them that we cared about their futures. And the donation meant that we brought with us needed funds for the orphanage to continue providing quality care to kids in need. That last one may have been our most important contribution of all.

So you might ask, why not just stay home and fundraise—and send the money we would have spent on airfare, too? It would certainly have been more efficient. But there was something else valuable about the trip: our own education as sheltered college students working however briefly far outside our comfort zones. Waking up under mosquito nets to the sound of roosters crowing, witnessing the challenges of rural poverty in a country that young Americans are more likely to visit as part of an all-inclusive resort package, hearing the ambitions of these children with such harrowing pasts...it changes how you look at your own life, and how you see the world around you.

I hope—I believe—that all of us volunteers boarded our plane back to the States at the end of that week with a strengthened commitment to help not just those in our own communities, but far away as well. So no matter how much of a difference we were able to make during our time in the Dominican Republic, I know we carried that with us—and acted on it in myriad ways—long after we got home to our comfortable beds and safe drinking water.

Service in College

If you've successfully instilled the habit, your teenagers likely will continue to volunteer after they head off to college. And, even if they haven't done much volunteering before college, they may get the bug when service projects become a bonding experience for dorm residents, fraternity and sorority members, athletic teams, special interest clubs, and other campus organizations. Some academic programs require students to intern with nonprofits in fields related to their course of study. Many colleges belong to Campus Compact, an organization that helps them develop community service and service learning projects. But some of the best projects spring up independently from students themselves. They see a need, gather others interested and, voila, a volunteer project is born.

TIP: *Idealist.org, a database of jobs at nonprofits, can help older teens and college students find internships, summer work or a first job after graduation. Opportunities for College Students—a section of Teach for America's website (teachforamerica.org)—lists volunteer opportunities with leading non-profit organizations that are committed to education and/or social change.*

From Julie

My sophomore year in college, I was looking for summer internship opportunities. I had been Googling nonprofit organizations without much direction when for some reason I thought of Heifer International. On their website, I stumbled upon descriptions of their Global Village educational farms, and the internship opportunities at those locations. At that point, I had already had several internships that were desk jobs. Thinking this would be a great opportunity to try something new, I applied to be an education/agriculture intern. In spite of the fact that I grew up in Washington, DC, and had almost never set foot on a farm, I was accepted. My first day at Overlook Farm in Massachusetts, I learned how to milk a goat, care for baby chicks and feed the pigs. I also slept in a tent, learned to harness and lead the water buffalo without being (too) intimidated and made friends with the other volunteers. Perhaps most challenging, I led educational programs for groups of all ages—from churches, summer camps, and colleges—to teach them about what life is like for the people Heifer works with around the globe. On a typical day, we would use a huge map to demonstrate food scarcity around the world, tour the farm and then cook lunch over an open flame in a house similar to one you would find in rural Thailand, Peru or Kenya. As an introverted city kid, I was WAY out of my comfort zone, in pretty much every way. And I ended up having one of the best summers of my life! I made so many wonderful friends, all interested in hunger and poverty issues and sustainable agriculture. And I discovered I was capable of a lot more than I would have thought. Even milking a goat.

PROFILE IN GENEROSITY:

A First Lady's Challenge

Community service got a big boost at George Washington University in the fall of 2009 when students invited new First Lady Michelle Obama to be their 2010 commencement speaker. She responded with a challenge: She'd speak if students completed 100,000 hours of service by the following May 1. By the time she took the stage at the May 16 graduation ceremony in Washington, DC, the students had racked up 163,980 hours. During her speech, Mrs. Obama noted that she was inspired by the monthly update letters about their tutoring children, working in a free medical clinic, restoring a high school, helping veterans, and dancing with residents at a senior citizens prom, to name just a few.[4]

---

[4] Washington Post, *May 17, 2010.*

TIP: *Is your college student involved in an exceptional community service project? Tell him or her about Generous U, an annual contest open to college campus groups nationwide. Entries are judged on YouTube videos plus essays describing the projects. The winning group receives the Sillerman Prize of $10,000, and their campus gets the honorary designation of Generous U to display on the college website. The competition is sponsored by Brandeis University's Sillerman Center for the Advancement of Philanthropy. (sillermancenter.brandeis.edu/prize).*

From Julie

As a college student with an ever-changing class and work schedule, I tended to mix things up with my volunteer commitments each semester. Collecting recyclables in my freshman dorm...reading with first graders at the local elementary school...helping out at a day center for disabled adults while studying abroad...there was always something to do.

One of my favorite volunteer gigs was at Literacy for Life, an adult learning center on my college's campus. The organization tutors adults who need help studying for the GED, learning basic computer skills or practicing English as a second language.

I was assigned to work with Volodomir, a 30-something immigrant from the Ukraine who worked for a local janitorial company cleaning hotels and businesses. Volodomir lived with other immigrants, and mostly spoke Ukrainian or Russian, so he wanted a chance to practice his English. We enjoyed getting to know each other a little more each week. Some weeks he would tell me about his opinions on the volatile political situation in his home country, or about his work as an accountant when he still lived in the Ukraine. Other weeks he asked me to help him learn the vocabulary he needed to take care of something going on in his life—such as explaining to a mechanic what was wrong with his car. I learned at least as much from him as he did from me.

College Courses in Philanthropy

Philanthropy classes are proliferating on college campuses, driven by Millennials who grew up performing community service and have developed a growing interest in careers in the nonprofit sector. In many of the courses, which combine the theory and practice of philanthropy, students study how nonprofits are funded and then give grants, usually with real funds. In some courses, students raise the grant monies themselves; in others, foundations provide the funds. Even if they don't end up working for nonprofits, the students still gain experience for their personal philanthropy.

Doris Buffett, philanthropist and sister of billionaire Warren Buffett, has had a major hand in some of these undergraduate courses. The Learning by Giving Foundation, a spinoff of her Sunshine Lady Foundation, provides grants to more than 35 undergraduate schools. Louise Sawyer, Learning by Giving's former academic director, designed and taught the course at Tufts University.

"Doris's goal was to sow the seeds of civic engagement and effective charitable giving in undergrads," Sawyer explained. "It's fabulous for students to be given responsibility for decision-making. It gives them an experience that changes lives. It's also wonderful for the community organizations that receive support, and colleges love it for the values it reinforces which are often in alignment with the college's mission. The beauty of teaching philanthropy is that it lends itself to many disciplines."

A Course for the Masses

The success of college philanthropy courses led the Learning by Giving Foundation to reach beyond the campuses. In partnership with Rebecca Riccio, director of the Social Impact Lab at Northeastern University, the foundation created the first massive open online course (MOOC) on philanthropy in 2013. The free course, called Giving With Purpose, taught 10,000 participants from all over the world how to identify effective nonprofits. During the lessons, philanthropists such and Doris and Warren Buffett, Baseball Hall of Famer Cal Ripken, Jr. and broadcaster Soledad O'Brien described their approaches to giving. As part of the course, students could nominate nonprofits for grants and then vote on which ones should receive a portion of $130,000 provided by the foundation and the university. The course was repeated in 2014 when $150,000 was divided among 30 U.S. nonprofits.

PROFILE IN GENEROSITY:

Philanthropy Class and Service Lead to a Career

Jen Bokoff had long been an active volunteer at her high school when she enrolled at Tufts University in 2004. "I planned to be a math major, but thought that doing some volunteering would help me still relate to people." At a freshman activities fair, she learned about LIFT, a one-stop community center where trained advocates, including mostly college students, help individuals to navigate personal, social and financial problems. Experience at LIFT led her to two different majors: sociology and community health.

But it was a course she took in her junior year that led her to a career path. Students enrolled in Experiments in Philanthropy learned about nonprofits and the foundations that fund them. Students were each assigned to work with a nonprofit in the community and to write a grant proposal on the organization's behalf. Then, the students— organized as two philanthropic boards—read each other's grant requests and decided which ones would share in $10,000 supplied by the Sunshine Lady Foundation. Bokoff enjoyed the class so much that she became a teaching assistant the following year. Her grant making experience led her to a position as a program officer for a private foundation. In 2013, she was named director of GrantCraft, a service of the Foundation Center in New York, the leading source of information about philanthropy worldwide.

"Experiential grantmaking can teach change in a whole new way," says Riccio, who leads the online class and also Northeastern's undergrad classes in philanthropy. "From cradle to grave, everyone's lives are tied up in the nonprofit sector. They are born in a hospital, go to museums, attend a university. Nonprofits are already an integral part of their lives, and yet they come to class thinking the nonprofit sector primarily serves the poor and disadvantaged. While that is a critical function, the nonprofit sector's role in society is far more complex." By teaching students philanthropy, "we empower them to see themselves as part of a system of social change."

PROFILE IN GENEROSITY:

Wendy Kopp's Big Idea

Several of Julie's friends, including one of her roommates, won coveted spots in Teach for America when they graduated from college. (It isn't easy to do; more than 57,000 individuals applied in 2013, for example, and only 6,000 were accepted.) It was their way of giving back, and give back they did. They worked hard for two years, often under frustrating conditions with limited classroom resources, to help provide quality education for kids growing up in low-income urban areas and rural communities.

Most remarkable is that the genesis of this huge movement was a college thesis written in 1989 by Princeton University student Wendy Kopp. Her professor called her idea "deranged." She proved him wrong when, by the following year, she had raised $2.5 million and founded the program with a charter corps of 500 committed recent college graduates.

Making Microloans Together

In a twist on classroom grantmaking, students in high schools and colleges around the globe are engaging in microfinance while learning about international issues, including poverty. In 2013, the website Kiva expanded its program of enabling individuals to make small loans to entrepreneurs trying to work their way out of poverty. Kiva partnered with financial services firm Citi to create Kiva U. The program offers a free curriculum and other resources for classrooms and clubs to learn about global problems and to address them, all while connected to other classrooms and clubs in an online community (kiva.org/kivau).

CHAPTER 8:

How Nonprofits and Businesses Fit In

We cannot always build the future for our youth,
but we can build our youth for the future.

President Franklin Delano Roosevelt

Nonprofits and businesses have a role to play in rearing the next generation of givers. They can be parents' allies—and they can benefit from playing that role.

Nonprofits that encourage family volunteering get children hooked early on their mission. These youngsters may be the organizations' future adult donors, volunteers and board members. These kids also may provide valuable volunteer help despite their young ages. They often bring their parents into the organizations' orbit, too. I've certainly become involved in organizations that Julie introduced me to.

Businesses benefit from appealing to families as well. Children have an influence on parents' buying decisions. They also grow up to be future employees. Millennials have already shown that they prefer to work for employers that practice corporate social responsibility. Today's children, Generation Z, are not far behind. It's advantageous to win their hearts when they are young.

How Nonprofits Can Engage Young People

Here are a few of the many ways nonprofits can engage children and families:

- Invite families in for site visits to get to know your work.

- Find ways families and young people—individuals or groups—can volunteer for you.

- Engage them through social media.

- Invite their input. Older teens can serve on ad hoc committees, advisory boards, even boards of directors.

- Offer internships.

- Cooperate with schools on community service and service learning activities.

TIP: *Volunteer Match (volunteermatch.org) not only lets organizations post volunteer jobs, but also offers free webinars, downloadable guides, videos and other resources to help nonprofits train and manage volunteers effectively.*

From Julie

Sometimes the most helpful volunteer project isn't the most exciting one. But savvy community organizations figure out how to make kids understand why what they're doing is important, even if it seems "boring" at first.

When I was a high school freshman, a few of my classmates and I spent a day volunteering at Friendship Place, a community outreach center for the homeless. What they needed our help with that day was the opposite of glamorous: power-washing the exterior of their building and stuffing envelopes. But before we jumped into our work, the staff member working with us that day gave a presentation on all the ways the organization helps our homeless neighbors.

She took us on a tour of the building, and we saw the storage area full of clean clothes available to those who come in needing them. She told us about the medical clinic they operate, so folks can come in off the street to get the care and medication they need. And she explained that though the work we would be doing that day wasn't the most exciting, it was important. Helping Friendship Place maintain the building would make it a more welcoming place for their homeless guests. And stuffing all those envelopes with letters to prospective donors would help them raise the money they needed to keep doing their good work.

By taking the time to explain the value of our volunteer time, she helped us feel excited to help in whatever way they needed us, even if what they needed help with wasn't the most exciting job on the planet.

Adapting to Child Volunteers

Many nonprofits welcome and appreciate youth volunteers. But the staffs of some nonprofits face an approach/avoidance conflict. Short-staffed organizations sometimes say managing adult volunteers is challenging enough. They may not see anything in their organization's work that lends itself to young volunteers, or they may think that involving kids in some jobs is too risky and exposes the organization to liability issues. If they do take youth volunteers, they many find it burdensome when desperate high schoolers call because they need a few more hours of community service to graduate and want the nonprofit to accommodate them instantly with some small assignment.

These concerns are legitimate. But they should not be deal breakers. With some creativity, many organizations can find ways to involve families and young people. For example, a service delivering meals to the homes of seriously ill people asked Julie's Brownie troop to decorate placemats and write holiday cards to their clients. Food pantries can't have little kids climbing on ladders to reach shelves, but the staff can identify safe jobs for young ones, such as packing food in paper bags while their parents supervise. Almost any nonprofit could use a tech-savvy teen to coach staffers in social media or to take photos and videos for the organization's website. Even young children can take photos. A staffer from a group that teaches sailing told me they had an event at which youngsters were given disposable cameras to capture the activities. She was delighted with the results, some of which were website-worthy. Since the photos were shot from child height, "they gave us a whole new angle from our usual photos."

The ideas are endless. If arranging jobs for young volunteers is too difficult for a small staff, perhaps an adult volunteer or board member would be willing to take charge.

Jenny Friedman, founder of Doing Good Together, said many nonprofits "are not focused on young people, especially not families with young kids." But once they have experience with young volunteers, she said, they tend to become more open. The organization develops a culture that's welcoming to the younger set. "It's surprising how effective young kids can be if they are organized well."

TIP: *GenerationOn, the youth service movement of Points of Light, offers a "Tool Kit for Family-Friendly Managed Projects" to help nonprofits engage young volunteers. Another valuable resource is the detailed guide—"Ready-Set-Go!"—which provides best practices and strategies to build an organization's capacity to engage family and youth volunteers. Both are free downloads at generationon.org.*

PROFILE IN GENEROSITY:

Moms Become "Philanthropy Event Planners"

Friends Alex Sklar and Lisa Geyer of Phoenix each have two young sons of the same ages. When their boys were 2 ½ and 5, the mothers began looking for volunteer projects that the families could do together.

"One of the biggest reasons we started thinking about volunteering with our children is because we feel so blessed," Geyer explained. "Our kids go to great schools and are surrounded by children who have a lot, and we wanted to show them the world outside their bubble. We wanted them to learn that some families have to worry about where their next meal is coming from or where they are going to sleep that night." The women figured that, if they started when their children were really young, "they'd grow up knowing that helping others is who we are, and this is what we do."

They started small. Their sons would pick out some of their gently used toys and books and take them to a homeless shelter, along with food to help stock the pantry. Their boys played on the shelter playground with residents' kids, learning that the children in the shelter aren't different from them, only their circumstances are.

Unfortunately, the mothers had a hard time finding nonprofits that welcomed families with young children. Many of their friends had the same dilemma, so in 2012, the two moms created Families Giving Back. Each month, they arrange two to four projects that Phoenix-area families can volunteer for. Their biggest challenge has been lining up the volunteer opportunities. "When we make the initial call to a nonprofit, the response might be, 'We can't have you here because of liability

issues,'" Geyer said. "Or they are maxed to capacity and don't have the
staff to handle it. They'll say they don't have time to figure out how to
work with kids. That's where Alex and I come in. We offer the ideas and
handle all the work. We're 'the philanthropy event planners.'"

Once the two mothers had built a track record of running
successful projects for a few nonprofits, they found it was easier to
sell the idea to others. And they were persistent. It took them a year
of phone calls and emails to get a meeting with the local Ronald
McDonald House (RMH), which has a rule that volunteers who
interact with families staying at the house must be at least 16. "We said,
okay, but here are some ways we can work around the restrictions. We
just have to get creative," Geyer said.

After the initial meeting, the RMH staff became excited about the
possibilities, and soon the women were running their first project. The
child volunteers, with help from their parents, decorated flower pots,
planted cactuses in them, and put them in front of each of the 45 doors
where families live while their children are being treated at the nearby
children's hospital. Then the volunteers took a tour with a staff member.
For their second project, the families brought supplies and assembled
250 hand-decorated welcome bags with toiletries and other goodies.
These are especially appreciated because families staying at RMH often
have to leave home in a hurry and don't remember to pack everything
they need.

The two friends created a website to promote the activities they
plan each month, always held on weekends. Families register online.
The number of families that can participate depends on the project.
A park cleanup may need a lot of volunteers while stocking a food
pantry might only have space for a small group. Every project has

a recommended minimum age. Some of their most popular events are book drives where families stock the shelves at the library of a homeless shelter. Work at food pantries is popular, too, because kids can relate to the idea of hunger and people needing food. "Families bring nonperishable items and leave the shelves fully stocked," Sklar said. Sometimes grandparents help, too.

The two women make it easy for nonprofits. "The only thing the nonprofit has to do is provide the space and maybe give us a tour," Sklar said. The women are careful to communicate with the families about rules, such as no picture taking to protect the privacy of the nonprofit's clients. They recommend a 1:1 adult to child ratio, and each family signs an annual volunteer waiver absolving Families Giving Back if a volunteer is hurt.

"We recommend that parents supervise but really let the kids do the work," Sklar said. "We've never had an issue of kids misbehaving or being a distraction to other volunteers. Everyone is very engaged and focused on their tasks!" The two moms run Families Giving Back as volunteers with no paid staff. They already have more requests than they can handle. They'd love to see their organization grow, but their goal is still personal. "We love that we can help other families, too," Sklar said, "but, at the end of the day, this is for our own kids."

TIP: *Even people who don't live in the Phoenix area will find useful information at familiesgivingback.org. The website's resources include suggested books for different ages to use as conversation starters and a list of at-home projects to benefit specific nonprofits in Phoenix, which can easily be replicated for nonprofits in other communities.*

What About Risk?

Many nonprofits shy away from engaging youth volunteers because of their fear of liability issues. The potential for risk shouldn't be the reason a nonprofit decides not to use youth as volunteers. Instead, it is something to address as part of any family and youth volunteer program. Nonprofits naturally want their activities to be as safe for volunteers as is reasonably possible. It's a good idea to brainstorm what could go wrong, how you would respond and what prevention measures to put in place to protect the staff, volunteers and the people you serve.

TIP: *Download the "Ready-Set-Go!" guide at generationon.org which covers managing risk. Another good source of information is the Nonprofit Risk Management Center (nonprofitrisk.org).*

Nonprofits Partnering with Schools

Schools with community service or service learning programs ought to partner with nonprofits. Some savvy nonprofits not only welcome these partnerships, but put specific information on their websites under their "Volunteer" tab to show their interest in students seeking service opportunities and the ways the organizations work with schools.

Youth on Nonprofit Committees...and Even Boards!

Having younger views on a committee or board can bring a fresh perspective, energy and creative ideas. Including the youth viewpoint in decision-making is especially important for organizations that provide services to youth. One place to start is with advisory committees. Nonprofits can invite young people who have already been engaged with the organization. It's better to bring on more than one at a time so the youth members don't feel like tokens and have a peer to relate to.

A tiny but growing number of nonprofits are even placing teenagers on their boards. The one limiting factor is state laws. In a few states, nonprofit board members have to be 21 or older, but in other states, the age begins at 18 and some at 16. The majority of states are silent on the issue.

Nonprofits should not underestimate young board members. I was once at a seminar on board governance when the issue came up. One attendee, who ran a United Way in the Midwest, had a teenage girl on his board. When board members were given personal fundraising goals for the annual drive, he told us, the teenager was exempted. To his amazement, she raised far more than most of her board colleagues. Apparently, it's hard for adults to turn down a teenager who is passionate about a cause.

Reach Them Where They Are

Nonprofits without a mobile communication strategy will not reach the next generation. The Digital Natives live on their phones and tablets. Nonprofits have to learn how to engage these youngsters online, and then induce them to take action. Tech-savvy adolescents can be helpful digital advisors to nonprofits. Some are even willing to help maintain social media sites. They can take photos for Instagram or shoot videos to post on YouTube, or perform other tasks to help an organization be creative—and effective—online.

TIP: *Two resources for nonprofits seeking to engage younger generations are the books* The Networked Nonprofit, *by Beth Kanter and Allison Fine, and* Cause for Change: The Why and How of Nonprofit Millennial Engagement *by Derrick Feldmann, who is the president of Achieve, a firm specializing in audience research and campaigns for nonprofits and businesses.*

PROFILE IN GENEROSITY:

A Teenage Nonprofit Consultant

Colton Strawser had some free time the summer after seventh grade. He heard about PCs For Youth, a small organization started by a high school sophomore. The nonprofit refurbished used computers and donated them to students who needed them to do their homework. "I can't fix a computer, but my family owned a business and I knew about marketing and customer service, so I volunteered," Strawser said. He Googled "grant-writing tips" and started raising money from foundations. By the time Strawser reached high school, the founder of PCs For Youth had graduated and Strawser became the volunteer executive director. The nonprofit's service area expanded from one county in Indiana to seven. Until he turned 16, "my poor mom had to drive me everywhere." The organization ran on a shoestring. "I was an extreme couponer when it came to office supplies. We were fortunate to get a bank to donate space and pay the electric bill." Gradually he began to get paid consulting work with nonprofits. His senior year, he took his courses online so he could become the development director for the La Grange County (Indiana) Council on Aging. He organized fundraising events, maintained the Council's social media pages and website, and produced a monthly newsletter. In 2013, he enrolled in Indiana University Lilly Family School of Philanthropy's philanthropic studies program while running his own nonprofit consulting business on the side.

Youth As Creators of Nonprofits

The United States has more than a million public charities, and the sector has been growing steadily. (Public charities are nonprofits that seek funding from the public.) Some people say the proliferation of nonprofits is not good because it fragments the sector, causing overlap in services and more competition for funds. Still, there are times when a new organization can serve a unique role.

Young people are often the creators of new nonprofits. The Millennial generation has been especially entrepreneurial, idealistic and socially conscious. Thanks to technology, they are also well-connected with like-minded people. Some start nonprofits because they have an idea for addressing a societal need and don't see anyone else doing it. With the help of adults, even school-age kids have created their own nonprofits. But doing so is not easy, what with the need for financial management, fundraising, staffing and hopping through legal hoops. Young people could incubate their projects in existing nonprofits that perform similar work. But not all nonprofits welcome new ventures or are willing to take risks on young people who may become impatient with bureaucracy. We hope that more nonprofits will be open to young people's engagement, and more young people will consider all options before deciding that a new stand-alone organization is the only way to go.

Businesses

Businesses, too, can help cultivate the next generation of givers. In earlier chapters of this book, we've noted companies that encourage youth volunteering. Even small businesses can help by joining with others. Here are a few more ideas:

- Organize a company-wide family volunteer day and find service projects suitable for children.
- Sponsor a contest to identify outstanding youth volunteers. Offer awards or even scholarships to the winners.

- Work with a school to host a philanthropy fair. (It looks like a science fair, with booths, posters and props, but instead of illustrating a science experiment, kids propose service projects and compete for small grants to execute their ideas.)

- Provide goods or services to community service projects organized by young people.

- Extend your employee matching gift program to include their children's donations to charity.

- Provide a pool of funds to a youth philanthropy group that teaches young people how to make grants.

TIP: *If you're a parent who works for or with a business or nonprofit or serves on a board, consider whether any of these ideas might apply, and bring them to the attention of the organization. In that way, you can help many other families and their children experience the joy of giving.*

CHAPTER 9:

The Gang's All Here: Giving Money with Others

It's not just about being able to write a check.
It's being able to touch somebody's life.

Oprah Winfrey

Mary Pat Alcus's family had just moved to Potomac, MD, when another mother in her sixth-grade daughter's school asked if they'd like to join a mother-daughter giving circle that was just starting. The concept was simple. Each of six families would contribute money to a pot and, after learning about many deserving organizations, the group would decide which charities would receive the donations. The children and adults contributed funds, some earned by the kids for doing chores. The giving circle members also volunteered at some of the places they funded. The club ended when the girls entered high school, and the last of the money was spent.

When Alcus's son hit sixth grade, he wanted to start a giving circle with his friends, too, having seen how much fun his sister had. Thus was born the Kid to Kid Giving Circle. Parents helped, but they let their kids take the lead. The circle became so popular that it eventually was opened to all of her son's classmates.

The Alcuses became part of a growing trend toward group giving by both adults and children. Working together on philanthropy is popular for two reasons: Shared learning can make for more informed decisions, and pooling money means donations have a bigger impact on the nonprofits. In the process, children learn about their community's needs and what the nonprofit sector does. They also gain skills, such as collaborating, making presentations and developing critical thinking. Some learn fundraising skills. And did we mention they have fun?

Group giving takes many forms and can be organized by parents, schools, religious congregations and foundations. It's even catching on in college classes where it becomes part of the curriculum (see Chapter 7). You don't have to be wealthy to get involved, because multiple people contribute to the donation pool. Some groups include both adults and children, and some are for children only—but with adults helping. Some are conducted totally online. Some are very informal, and others have bylaws and agendas.

TIP: *A giving circle can be strictly a family affair, with children and their parents, grandparents or other relatives making decisions together. See Chapter 3 to learn how to create a dinner table foundation.*

A more formal type of group giving is a youth philanthropy council or similarly named group, sponsored by an institution, often with funds provided by a foundation. Sometimes the youth raise all or a portion of the funds themselves. Participants—usually high schoolers, but sometimes middle schoolers—learn to assess their community's needs, evaluate nonprofits that are addressing those needs, and make decisions about where their grants would have the most impact. Your area may have such a council where your son or daughter could serve. Here are places to look.

Community Foundations

Most cities and many small towns have community foundations that pool donors' money and make grants to address community needs. There are more than 700 in the United States. Many sponsor giving circles for adults, and some have youth grantmaking opportunities or engage young philanthropists in other ways. Some community foundations run their own youth philanthropy groups while others partner with schools or other organizations.

The Noble County Community Foundation of Ligonier, IL, for example, has a group called P.U.L.S.E. (Philanthropists Utilizing Lifelong Service and Education) that draws a handful of 8th to 12th graders from each of five schools in the county. The group meets monthly to make grants to community organizations; the grant money and training support are provided by the Dekko Foundation, a family foundation committed to youth philanthropy. Noble County also has a program called Teens on Board that trains high school sophomores and juniors for service on nonprofit boards such as the library, animal shelter, parks department, food pantry and United Way.

TIP: *Community foundations in Michigan are pros when it comes to running youth philanthropy groups. That's because, in the 1990s, the Kellogg Foundation provided financial support for the Michigan Community Foundations' Youth Project. Adding locally raised matching money, more than 80 community foundations across the state created permanently endowed youth funds with Youth Advisory Councils in charge of the grantmaking. The Council of Michigan Foundations website has a guide and best practices for starting a youth grant making council (michiganfoundations.org/youth).*

Another way community foundations help families is through donor advised funds. The DAF is a charitable vehicle through which you donate money, receive an immediate tax deduction, and later choose which nonprofits you'd like to support. Other public charities and some large investment firms offer the vehicle as well, but community foundations are noted for providing special services for families that want to engage their children. For example, some provide information about local charities that appeal to children or take families on site visits. Sometimes grandparents set up donor advised funds as a way to work with their grandchildren on giving. Community foundations typically require a minimum amount to set up a fund. Contact the one in your area if you want more details about this giving vehicle. (cof.org/community-foundation-locator)

TIP: *The Community Foundation for Greater Atlanta engages the children of donor families in a program called Planet Philanthropy. The children of donors with advised funds are invited to a half-day program to learn about philanthropy. The Planet Philanthropy guidebook is useful for any parent interested in teaching children about giving. Download it and other helpful resources free at cfgreateratlanta.org.*

Jewish Teen Philanthropy

The number of youth philanthropy groups for Jewish teens has been growing rapidly. Often, youth are engaged in a grant-making group around age 13 when they have their bar or bat mitzvahs and can pool their cash gifts. There are also groups in summer camps, Jewish community centers and day schools. The Jewish Teen Funders Network (jtfn.org) has some excellent resources on how to organize teen philanthropy groups, including some that are suitable for nonreligious organizations.

Family Foundations

Family foundations can play two roles in training the next generation of givers. One is as a training ground for the young people in their own families. If a foundation is going to continue into the future, new generations must be prepared to take the place of the older family members. Some foundations create next gen boards, sometimes called junior boards, to provide training in grantmaking.

The second role is funding the kind of youth philanthropy programs described in this chapter. For youth to make grants, they need money. The adults helping the youth need training. Some family foundations fund those needs and make it possible for kids from families without wealth to have philanthropic experiences.

The Highland Street Foundation in Boston is a good example. It partners with schools and community organizations, such as Boys and Girls Clubs, to teach small groups of students how to evaluate nonprofits in their community. They make site visits, present the findings to the group, decide together how to allocate the grants, then attend an award ceremony during which they hand checks to the nonprofits selected.

The George Foundation in Richmond, TX, runs a program for 175 high school juniors and seniors each academic year, in partnership with area schools, the Chamber of Commerce, businesses and nonprofits. The students work on a variety of volunteer projects designed by local nonprofits. Through their volunteer experiences, the students become better equipped to determine monetary awards for the nonprofits. The year culminates in a spring luncheon attended by approximately 800 people where the nonprofits receive their grants, and scholarships are awarded to students.

The Burton D. Morgan Foundation in Hudson, OH, has funded several youth entrepreneurship and philanthropy-focused projects over the years. A rather unusual one was a collaboration with a school and a retirement community. The foundation paid for a training program used by a middle school teacher to prepare her students for grantmaking, then provided a fund so the students could work with the senior citizens to make grants. The seniors received training as well. The grantmaking process provided a learning experience for both age groups.

TIP: *The National Center for Family Philanthropy (ncfp.org) has many resources for families wishing to engage their younger members in the family's formal philanthropy. One of the best for family foundations and donor advised funds is "Igniting the Spark: Creating Effective Next Generation Boards," which is a free download. The center produced the publication in a joint project with Youth Philanthropy Connect, a project of the Frieda C. Fox Foundation. YPC hosts* *conferences for youth from next gen boards and provides other resources (youthphilanthropyconnect.org). The nonprofit consulting practice 21/64 (2164.net), a project of the Andrea and Charles Bronfman Philanthropies, offers many resources to help multi-generation families work together.*

CHAPTER 10:

Make it a Tradition

Life's persistent and most urgent question is
'What are you doing for others?'

Martin Luther King, Jr.

Children—and adults, too!—love traditions. Celebrating events or holidays in certain ways creates memories kids remember all their lives. Families can be quite definite about the way traditions should be adhered to. If you don't believe me, try making changes to the menu for your Thanksgiving dinner.

Celebrations, observances and holidays aren't just for making memories. They can also be ways to inspire your children to give. Get out a calendar, brainstorm ideas with them and mark some dates on which you'll create giving traditions.

When we think of acts of kindness, the focus is often the year-end November and December holidays. But giving can and should be embraced throughout the year. This is especially true because charities are often inundated with helpers near Christmas and would prefer to have more help in their traditionally slow months.

TIP: *Work with your kids to create a monthly "giving" calendar. Create your own "generosity days" or pick some holidays from the list below. Then jot down giving activities you plan to engage in, and let the kids add little drawings or photos cut out of magazines. For example, for September 28, National Good Neighbor Day, you could draw some leaves and plan to rake the yard of an elderly neighbor.*

143

Here are some observances and holidays to get you started:

JANUARY

Martin Luther King, Jr. Day

The civil rights leader's birthday is commemorated each year with the MLK Day of Service organized by the Corporation for National and Community Service, a federal agency that helps Americans improve the lives of their fellow citizens through service. Go to nationalservice.gov for ideas plus an online locator to find a local project you can join.

FEBRUARY

Valentine's Day

This is the perfect day to send homemade cards or take cookies to someone who is sick, in a nursing home or just generally in need of a little boost. You might also send valentine treats to our military men and women.

MARCH

Bake Sale No Kid Hungry

"You Can Bake a Difference" is a slogan for this popular event (formerly known as the Great American Bake Sale), which raises funds to help end childhood hunger. A project of Share Our Strength, the annual bake sale has a kid-friendly website where you can learn how to host your own sale or find one in your area to join. (nokidhungry.org)

Read Across America

Usually held March 2, which is Theodor Geisel's (Dr. Seuss's) birthday, this national event is sponsored by the National Education Association to promote reading to children. Here are a few ways young people can celebrate the joy of reading: donate books to school libraries; collect gently used books for children in homeless shelters; read to younger kids in after-school programs. You can read Dr. Seuss books, such as *The Grinch Who Stole Christmas*, to your younger kids and discuss the generosity themes.

APRIL

Global Youth Service Day

Youth Service America sponsors this, the largest service event in the world and the only one that's focused on helping youth volunteers to address the planet's most critical issues and to change their own communities. To find out the upcoming dates, visit www.gysd.org.

National Siblings Day

Take a break from sibling rivalry on April 10, and get kids to think of something to do that celebrates their relationship with brothers and sisters.

Earth Day

Held annually on April 22, Earth Day promotes taking action to solve the earth's environmental problems.

Digital Deed: **On the 40th anniversary in 2010, the Earth Day Network launched a campaign called A Billion Acts of Green®, with the goal of registering one billion actions in advance of the United Nations Conference on Sustainable Development in June 2012. By Earth Day that year, the goal had already been reached. Now, they're trying for the next billion, focusing on specific, timely issues. Go to earthday.org to add your action.**

Arbor Day

In most states, Arbor Day is the last Friday in April. A few places use different dates depending on the best tree planting times. Observe this day by planting a tree, perhaps in honor of a friend, a family member or even a beloved pet. You can plant a tree in your own yard or join an effort to plant trees in public spaces.

To get in the mood, read Dr. Seuss's *The Lorax*, or watch the movie and discuss with your kids the importance of trees. Ask them what trees do: produce fruit and nuts, provide shade to cool your home, offer shelter for birds and other wildlife and purify the air, for example.

 **Digital Deed:** At the Arbor Day Foundation website (arborday.org), you can buy Give-A-Tree® cards for any occasion. They'll send you the card so you can sign it and give it to someone you wish to honor. Inside is the message: "In your honor, a tree is being planted in a National Forest."

MAY

May Day

Preserve the tradition of this May 1 celebration of spring by making small baskets, filling them with candy or flowers and delivering them to neighbors' doorsteps anonymously.

Mother's Day

Suggest kids figure out something to do for or with Mom in lieu of buying a gift. Kids can also volunteer at their mother's favorite nonprofit or make a donation in her name. Think, too, about how to help other mothers. Do something nice with a mom in your neighborhood whose own kids live far away, for example.

From Julie

I was born in summer, 1985. Around my birth date, my dad noticed a pin oak seedling about five inches high that had sprouted from an acorn in our tiny urban backyard. We get those every year, and my mom usually pulled them up, but this one was in a perfect spot where it had room to grow. Today, 29 years later, the tree is enormous—at least 50 feet tall—and shades the entire yard. My parents put a little plaque at the base, naming it "Julie's Tree." It definitely proves the adage "Mighty oaks from little acorns grow."

JUNE

Father's Day

Using Mother's Day as the model, encourage your older children and help your younger ones to brainstorm ways to honor their own dad and maybe someone else's, as well.

JULY

Independence Day

Get patriotic. Help make America beautiful by volunteering to clean up a park, for example.

AUGUST

Anything Can Happen Day

We Boomers who were fans of the Mickey Mouse Club loved the idea of a day when the unexpected happened. Here's where your kids can get really creative. Pick a day in August and let them make up a giving holiday. They could call it Pay it Forward Day and make a list of small deeds they could do for others as a surprise. Or, they could think of ways to incorporate giving into one day of your family's summer vacation. Maybe the date could be linked to going back to school—such as holding a drive to collect school supplies and backpacks for children in need.

SEPTEMBER

National Day of Service and Remembrance

In 2009, Congress designated September 11 as a day for service in honor of the victims of the 2001 terrorist attacks and gave the Corporation for National and Community Service the responsibility for supporting the effort. There is a search function on the website (nationalservice.gov) to help you find a service project in your community.

Grandparents Day

On the first Sunday after Labor Day, children can celebrate their grandparents by sending them cards, photos and handmade crafts; making a donation in the grandparents' names to their favorite charity; or offering to help them brush up on their technology skills. Consider adopting a grandparent, too—an elderly neighbor who'd appreciate visits, baked goods or help with yard work.

National Good Neighbor Day

This annual observance on September 28 is a great time for families to do good deeds for neighbors who need help or to organize a neighborhood clean-up project. Children can hold a yard sale and donate a portion of their profits to charity. Or the kids could organize the entertainment for a block party and set the price of admission as canned food and gently used clothes for a homeless shelter.

OCTOBER

Make a Difference Day

Sponsored by 3 and Points of Light, this national day of community service is held annually on the last Saturday in October. The website (makeadifferenceday.com) has project ideas and resources. If you want to join someone else's project, enter your zip code to find one near you.

From Julie

Make a Difference Day was huge at my college. Hundreds of us would fan out into the community to help with all kinds of projects such as landscaping the gardens at the local elementary school, helping set up local nonprofits' fall festivals or painting classrooms at a day care center. Joining a group project is a great way to have a big impact in just one day and meet other people who love to volunteer.

Halloween

Have your kids Trick or Treat for UNICEF while they go door to door collecting candy. You can order a free collection box or print out a canister wrap to tape on your own container at the website youth.unicefusa.org/trickortreat. The site also provides additional ideas for fundraising online or throwing fundraising parties.

Need a costume idea? One year our young neighbor Martha came dressed as a UNICEF box! We've also had Trick or Treaters who were collecting candy for troops overseas through Operation Gratitude (operationgratitude.com).

TIP: *In mid-October, a Girl Scout troop in our neighborhood holds a Halloween costume drive for an organization providing services to homeless children. People with new or gently used non-violent costumes can drop them off on a Scout family's porch prior to Halloween. This would be an easy project for any family to organize.*

NOVEMBER

Family Volunteer Day

The Saturday before Thanksgiving is a day designated for families to volunteer together. It was started more than two decades ago by Points of Light. You can download a project guide at generationOn.org to get ideas for activities for all ages and to learn more about family volunteering.

Thanksgiving

This is it: THE day to think and talk about what your family is grateful for and to find ways to demonstrate that gratitude. Introduce this as a dinner table conversation topic in early November so your children have plenty of time to come up with ideas.

Giving Tuesday

After the shopping frenzy of Black Friday and CyberMonday, go online on Giving Tuesday to put the giving back in your holiday season. See Chapter 4 for details.

DECEMBER

Christmas, Hanukkah, Kwanzaa

Regardless of how your family celebrates these holidays, make time for giving traditions—caroling at nursing homes; filling food baskets; collecting socks, mittens and warm clothing for the homeless; donating to Toys for Tots; shopping for a needy child from a Salvation Army Angel Tree...opportunities for giving abound. Provide ideas, but let your children take the lead on deciding what you'll do. Older children may want to include their friends in some of the activities, too.

What about all the other days?

Some states have their own holidays, to honor historic events for example. Since those sometimes involve a day off from work and school, you could use that time as an additional opportunity for volunteering. Once you have blocked out your calendar with the national and state holidays, then put in your personal family celebrations— such as birthdays, bar and bat mitzvahs, graduations, weddings and anniversaries, any of which can have a charitable component. You'll find ideas for many of these celebrations in previous chapters. Happy holidays!

ACKNOWLEDGEMENTS

Many individuals had a hand in helping make this book a reality. First, I want to thank the many people who provided guidance or granted interviews, especially Mary Pat Alcus, Lois Baron, Jen Bokoff, Rob Collier, Steve Culbertson, Emily Davis, Skye DeLano, Maya Enista, Derrick Feldmann, Aria Finger, Jenny Friedman, Mary Galeti, Lisa Geyer, Laura Giadorou-Koch, Beth Kanter, Deborah Hoover, Heather Jack, Amy Johnson, Claudia Jacobs, Joe Kahne, Dee Koch, Rebecca Riccio, Kathy Saulitis, Louise Sawyer, Sara Schiarer, Aaron Sherinian, Alexa Sklar, Jules Spector, Colton Strawser, Jody Vara, Lana Volftsun and Stefanie Zelkind.

I also extend sincere thanks to Annie Hernandez, Sharna Goldseker and Lisa Parker, friends who have been steadfast supporters, especially providing me with insights into the world of youth philanthropy. Char Mollison, Karen Green and Ginny Esposito have not only been philanthropy mentors but have supported my career and been true friends to me over many years.

I have benefitted from knowing some wonderful writers, good friends all, who have cheered me on in countless ways both professionally and personally, particularly Elise Ford, Kathy McKay, Cheryl Aubin, Sarita Venkat, Heather Taylor, Bobbi Conner and all the members of the Writer Moms.

I am sincerely grateful for longtime friends and colleagues Tina Dokken, who edited the manuscript, and Brenda Hawkes, who created an excellent design for it.

Finally, I am grateful to my husband Tom Price, a freelance journalist, who read early drafts and offered much good advice, and my daughter Julie, who agreed to lend her own stories and a younger generation's perspective to the book. I couldn't have written it without both of you.

—Susan Crites Price

CPSIA information can be obtained at www.ICGtesting.com
Printed in the USA
LVOW10s1018181115

463133LV00001B/28/P